Praise for
Shamus A'Rabbitt

"I am inclined to hail Shamus as the many sided Franklin of
the twentieth century, after seeing how easily he flits from
metallurgy to the light fantastic chronicles of the doings
of the Chinese 'boys' and their 'masters' and 'missies.' The
Ballads may also be a study for the future investigator of
pidgin English."

William Henry Chamberlin,
Chief Far East Correspondent, *Christian Science Monitor*

"The delightful 'Ballads of the East' . . . we followed one
another about the house reading aloud that about the cook
who cooked for two families, 'the Minute Man in Shanghai,'
and other gems which for the time being make us hungry
for the 'love and friendship of the rovers overseas.' We find
the selection perfect."

Jim Howe,
Formerly *AP* Correspondent in China and Japan

"I have read the 'Ballads' at a sitting and chuckled over it.
It is easy reading, as some faces are easy to look at . . . If I
were writing a review, I would start by saying that for once
I had found a Publisher who spoke true on the cover of his
wares."

Hugh Byas,
Tokyo Correspondent *London Times, New York Times*

brevities aplenty. . . . sparkling epigrammatic wit. . . . neat vignettes of the ports and their types and life. . . . earthy, unpretentious; written by a roamer, for himself and other roamers who demand not anaemic food for the brain but seasoned sustenance for the soul.

". . . he carries with him ever-fresh these priceless first impressions which, being a poet, he was able to record in entertaining rhyme.

". . . They are redolent of the atmosphere. . . . when China was China. . . . archaically quaint for the old-timer a gift of the past that he thought he had lost in sprightly jingling phrases and a lucky red cover."

Jaberu,
South China Morning Post

"Ten to fifteen years ago our readers were delighted by the versifying of a young American who wrote under a pseudonym . . . concealing the identity of Mr. Shamus A'Rabbitt. Pleasing, forcible and highly individual, the poems. . . . had a unique appeal in their subtle conveyance of the glamour and atmosphere of the Orient . . . his poetic efforts have a leisurely humour and mellow wisdom that makes them valuable, while Sapajou has put them into an environment that imparts a distinctly new relish."

W. J. K.
The China Mail

"An amusing volume from the pen of Shamus A'Rabbitt . . .
The author. . . . has a keen understanding of the Oriental
scene and is a talented writer of verse. . . . The majority of
the subjects will be found of real interest to all readers of
English who live in the East and should be even more so to
Old China Hands who have departed after long residence
here, as the perusal of but a few lines will recall all the
glamour and color for which the Orient is so well known."

A. O. B.

The China Press

"Illustrated by Sapajou, Shamus A'Rabbitt's already much
appreciated light verse has here been collected in an
attractive volume for those who would like to show their
friends at home that despite present troubles people in
China can still look on the funny side of life. Mr. A'Rabbitt
knows his East and also his club bar — and Sapajou manfully
assists him in his exposition."

E. H.

The North China Daily News

"Mr. A'Rabbitt. . . . is generally regarded as an engineer or
scientist. But in fact he is more than all that. He is a wide
traveller to begin with, a philosopher, a humorist. . . . His
ballads are full of wisdom and humor."

Japan Times & Mail

"Mr. A'Rabbitt — almost unbelievably this is not a Pen-
name — has an impish sense of humour."

Japan Chronicle

"An engineer and a chemist, Mr. A'Rabbitt has lived in China and Japan for over three decades and his writing shows that he has viewed the varied Oriental scene as a philosopher and something of a critic. . . . the ballads now make their bow in collected form, and much will be the delight of those who read them. They are redolent of the atmosphere of the East. Ingenious rhyming is combined with humour and wisdom, and there is a charm about the book which will instantly appeal. Many drawings by Sapajou give interpretation as well as illustration."

Shanghai Sunday Times

"Shamus A'Rabbitt. . . has scored again. . . The writer. . . has concocted a barrel of fun for those who are familiar with the China scene of a few years back—The poems are peculiar to the writer and so catch much of his own individualism. Some of the best of them have an epigrammatic quality, something for which the poet is well known. . . Because Shamus A'Rabbitt wrote by impulsion more than compulsion, the poems have a pep and freshness not always to be found in newspaper poetry."

Adrienne Moore,
The Japan Advertiser

"In the din of warfare when opposing forces are at each others' throats and the blasts of bombs, and shell-fire explosions benumb the senses of humankind, it is a welcome relief to become conscious of a kindlier, pleasanter note, a happy overtone in the general discord, that gives assurance that the whole balance of normal things is not yet overturned, and that mirth and laughter have not gone wholly out of modern life. This gracious alleviation comes in the form of a little book of verse, Ballads of the East by a gifted writer. . . . The author has lived in China and Japan for more than three decades, and he has observed the colorful and varied panorama of Oriental life with keen understanding and ever kindly sympathy. . . . At intervals through the years have bits of his verse appeared in print, formerly in the Hongkong newspapers and occasionally in other publications, under the pen name of John Kyoto. . . . Shamus A'Rabbitt, whatever else he may be, is a poet philosopher, and assuredly, he knows the East and the lives of those from overseas who have chosen to cast their lot in this part of the world. There is a glint of impish mischief, whimsical understanding and mellow wisdom in the lilt and flow of his lines. His writing is terse and full to the brim of the zest of living, and he has a singular genius for terseness, often presenting intricate thought forms in sparkling phrases, at times in single words."

C. J. L.

The Far Eastern Review

"Mr. Rabbitt touches with gentle humor, life in the East and those who have heard its call will delight in these verses from the introductory one and the second 'The Lure of the East ' to the last line pausing to reread and chuckle with delight over the well depicted aspects of life on the China coast. Not only does he deal with the servant problem and pictures of tropical life and far eastern travel but he touches the heart of all overseas folk in 'The Mail '."

M. C.

The China Weekly Review

CHINA RHYMES

Two classics of Old China Coast poetry

Shamus A'Rabbitt

Illustrations by "Sapajou"

First Published in 1937 & 1938

With a New Foreword

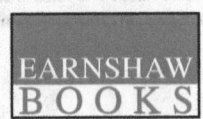

EARNSHAW BOOKS

China Rhymes

By Shamus A'Rabbitt

With a foreword by Andrew Chubb

ISBN-13: 978-988-18154-3-9

Ballads of the East was first published in 1937 by Hagar.
China Coast Ballads was first published in 1938 by Willow Pattern Press.
This edition with a new foreword is published by

This book has been reset in 10pt Book Antiqua. Spellings and punctuations are left as in the original edition.

EB016

Published by Earnshaw Books Ltd. (Hong Kong)

FOREWORD
By Andrew Chubb

IT'S A SWELTERING, muggy night and the mosquitoes are dancing around your whisky soda. A wafting drain-smell assails your nose; you set down your glass next to the pen and paper on the rattan table beside you. "Boy!" you call out. "Catchee pipe chop chop!" You pick up the pen and paper.

Shamus A'Rabbitt was the pseudonym (the *Japan Chronicle* was surely joking when it expressed belief to the contrary) of James Aloysius Rabbitt, an American engineer who spent most of the years between World Wars I and II working in China and Japan. He published and lectured widely on metallurgy and industry in East Asia, as well as on tea, rice, silk and Japanese history.

Mr Rabbitt (1877-1969) signed an agreement in 1921 with Dr Sun Yat-sen to help with harbor developments around the city of Canton, now generally called Guangzhou, and spent the next few years as a consultant engineer on other dockyard and railway projects around China. He served as commercial attaché at the US embassy in Tokyo, then spent a while in the US before returning to Japan in 1932, this time as an adviser to the Japanese Bureau of Information on Nickel.

The 1930s were a rather sensitive time for an

American – or indeed a China Hand – to be helping Japan with the production of metals. The Japanese had occupied Manchuria and were pushing into northern China and threatening Shanghai. But while Mr Rabbitt clearly loved Japan, during World War II he brought his knowledge of the enemy to Washington's Panel of Far Eastern Experts.

Between his departure from Japan in 1936 and the start of American involvement in the War, Mr Rabbitt returned to China, probably to Hong Kong, and published *Ballads of the East* through Shanghai adman and publisher A.R. Hager in 1937. A tiny collection of just 50 pages and 35 poems, some of which had previously appeared in newspapers like the *South China Morning Post*, *Japan Times* and *China Mail*, the *Ballads* appear to have been selected with publisher and audience in mind, as Mr Rabbitt reined in his obsession with the Land of the Rising Sun to concentrate on China.

The meaning of the title, a reference to the 'Ballad of East and West' by the then recently-departed Rudyard Kipling, runs a little deeper than it might at first appear. Mr Rabbitt, from his perspective of involvement with major industry and infrastructure projects in China and Japan, was in a position to correct Kipling's famous lament, "Oh, East is East and West is West, and never the twain shall meet." His hopes for a future of East-West cooperation through industry – along with a genial rebuke for his esteemed predecessor – are heard in *Ballads* in 'East and West'. But given the industrialism and technology which were fundamental to the

Japanese militarists' growing reign of terror in China as well as the looming war in Europe, Mr Rabbitt was right to retain a degree of ambivalence and skepticism about technology, as seen in the poems 'Our Synthetic World' and 'In Defence of Nothing'.

Rather than dwell on the darker questions of colonialism and mechanical warfare, however, these ballads were created to make fun of the world of the white man in China, the snobs, society fools, haughty ladies and various kinds of hypocrites and pretenders. The pitiful pettiness of even having a social ladder, let alone trying to climb one, in an overseas community of a few thousand people provided a rich source of mirth and material to the part-time poet. Also, the absurd, concomitant notion that even the lowest members of the foreign community should live like kings jarred with the reality that Mr Rabbitt comments on in 'The Call of the East' and elsewhere: that many were in fact degenerates who relied on servants even to tie their shoelaces.

The fact that the people buying the book were the very ones being mocked didn't stop the first *Ballads* becoming a huge hit in the foreign communities on both sides of the Sea of Japan. Readers possibly recognized those around them in the outrageous characters without seeing themselves – Mr Rabbitt actually alludes to this phenomenon in 'The Other Fellow' and elsewhere – or perhaps they were simply charmed by the author's own self-effacing identification of himself among those he satirized. Although Mr Rabbitt was 60

years old when *Ballads* was released, and the earliest
dated poem is from 1923, when he was 46, his characters
range all the way from young bachelor/griffins and
society daughters through to senile taipans and aging
spinsters.

So by popular demand, Shamus A'Rabbitt returned
the following year, 1938, with the larger *China
Coast Ballads*. While continuing to poke fun at the
idiosyncrasies of the foreigners, the structure of *China
Coast Ballads* roughly sees the author journeying up and
down the China coast, from Hong Kong to Canton, to
Nanning, Shanghai and up the Yangtze, to Peking and
Manchuria and eventually to America via Japan.

These ballads do much more than poke fun: they
recreate, as only poetry can, a sense of place. The lyrics
on their own would have sufficed, but something of the
essence of the treaty port world comes through in the
"music", so to speak. They fairly demand to be read at
a chaotically full-throttle pace, in a single sitting even,
just as New York and London *Times* correspondent
Hugh Byas professed to have done. The peppy,
limerick-like rhythms draw you in and then whirl you
through the sights and smells, just like an overzealous
tour guide on the Bund. In fact, reading the *Ballads*
feels like nothing so much as getting a guided tour
– not only of the tourist spots, but of local society. For
busy people with little room in their schedules for a
visit to Old China, there could be no better guide than
Shamus A'Rabbitt.

Mr. Rabbitt's compendious wit often sums up whole

concepts in a single line (Old Cathay, "Where centuries pass as though a day") or even, having laid out the background, in a word ("Maskee!"). The latter skewers the overarching day-to-day background of scribbled chits, fast cash and easy debt. The picture is filled out with plenty of short pieces depicting the hilarious minutiae of the treaty port – Missie (white woman) at the Chinese butcher's shop, the desperate wait for the mail, drunken sailors on shore leave, undersized newspapers, ever-present liquor and occasional homesickness. But it is not that the picture rendered is so elaborate, it is that the words, rhyme and meter combine to evoke a feeling almost of time-travel.

Witnessing the dynamic China of the early 21st century is a privilege, but the flipside is that it is now rare to see human activity without the involvement of modern machinery of some kind. Even in poor, remote corners of China there always seems to be a reckless motorbike zooming around the mountain, or an overloaded three-wheeler hauling hay from the fields. In Mr Rabbitt's time, however, those foreigners who deigned to leave their concession-bubbles and observe the countryside found a world unchanged for millennia, something many of them recognized as amazing, among them, of course, James A. Rabbitt. Like many writers before him, Mr Rabbitt expresses complete awe at China's 'celestial' landscapes and civilization, which he likens to love in its timeless constancy and to the Milky Way in its staggering abundance ('Desert Dreams').

Although there are brief, beautiful moments of contemplation and melancholy ('At Anchor', 'Shadows') and the occasional swashbuckling sea shanties ('Night Boat to Canton', 'The Typhoon'), with the great Sapajou's cartoons in accompaniment, comedy is never more than a page away. Mr Rabbitt was unafraid to use humor to confront the darker side of the European's world in the East. The fate of the small-town religious kid in 'Innocents in the East' speaks loudly of the decadence and vice he sees underlying the vast web of moneymaking, concluding that no-one could survive there with their innocence intact. It is far from black humor, but it complements perfectly the lightness of 'Maskee!' on essentially the same issue.

'The Sanctimonious Griffin' lampoons the futility of the missionary efforts in China, another theme common in the writings of China Hands but one that was never expressed so succinctly or hilariously. Meanwhile, the final line of 'Go Ye Forth and Preach the Gospel' nails the cynical exploitation of missionaries for political purposes. Though Mr Rabbitt doesn't make his politics clear in his poems, he is equally merciless in his treatment of snobs and of their victims, the snubbed. And in roasting the hypocrisy and snobbishness he sees at 'The Humane Society Ball' (among other such gatherings) he makes something of a stand in favor of the Chinese.

In stark contrast to his almost burlesque treatment of his foreigner peers, the Chinese are, in perfect sync with Sapajou's cartoons, always represented as good-natured and honest – if a tad simple. But how else could it have been, given that their words are all rendered in Pidgin English? In truth, beyond the short, endearing pieces on the boys, amahs and cooks that were essential to the foreigners' world, locals rarely figure prominently. Mr Rabbitt didn't appear to speak much Chinese, although his addition of words to the Hong Kong sailors' shanty he hears in 'When We Go Sailing Home' is brilliant. But he couldn't have rendered any other world as sumptuously as he did his own world – the world of Shamus A'Rabbitt.

Judging by the place of his death at 92 years old – at his home in the US Virgin Islands – James A. Rabbitt did rather well in life. But while it was surely not his two obscure books of verse that made him a wealthy man, it is hoped that republishing them will help ensure that his poetry is remembered.

Andrew Chubb
June 2009

Contents

GLOSSARY   XXII

BALLADS OF THE EAST

PROLOGUE   3
LURE OF THE EAST, THE   4
MARCO POLO   6
CALL OF THE EAST, THE   10
MASKEE!   12
SNUB, SNOBS AND SNOBBERY   14
HONGKONG JAZZ   19
CHANGEZ VOUS DAMES   21
SHADOWS   22
HONESTY   23
JEWEL, THE   24
ONE HEAD AND A DOUBLE THOUGHT   25
PASSION IN THE KITCHEN   26
CELESTIAL VINTAGE   27
PAYMASTER, THE   28
HOW   29
EAST AND WEST   30
CHINESE JOSS   31
MINUTE MAN IN SHANGHAI, THE   32
DEVIL'S RAILWAYS, THE   34
IGA LANG TANG   36
HENPECKED HUSBANDS OF CHIKIANG, THE   38

Rain, Rain, Beautiful Rain	40
Progress	43
Man Of Clay, A	44
Watch Your Step	46
Virtue Rewarded	47
White Nights	49
Dusky But True	51
Canton River, The	52
Humane Society Ball	56
Typhoon, The	58
King O'sliameen, The	60
Mail, The	62
God Save Our Trees	65

CHINA COAST BALLADS

PROLOGUE	75
IN THE EAST	76
THE GODDESS QUENCH	78
THE MYSTIC CITY	80
INNOCENTS IN THE EAST	81
DANCING PRINCESSES OF HONGKONG	83
A FAR EASTERN VARIETY	86
TO SIGN OR NOT TO SIGN	88
THE ABSENT MINDED SPORT	92
AS THE BETTER HALF THINKETH	95
THE SLACKER	99
SHORE LEAVE	102
NIGHT BOAT FROM HONGKONG TO CANTON	106
AT ANCHOR	110
THE SANCTIMONIOUS GRIFFIN	113
NEPTUNE'S DAUGHTER	115
SHADOWS	120
DREAMING ON THE WAY TO OLD NANNING	112
"GO YE FORTH AND SPREAD THE GOSPEL"	124
THE OTHER FELLOW	126
HOW DO YOU READ YOUR PAPER?	128
THE CALL PRIMEVAL	131
PREDIGESTINATION	132
THE ARCHEOLOGIST OF THE BREAKFAST TABLE	133
ADVENTURE	135
WANTED: A NAME!	136
SPARE THE TREES	137
DIGNITY	140
NERO THE HERO	142

TROPICAL ECSTASY 143
ABSENCE 144
EXILES 146
THE FAMILY SHRINE 147
DREAMLINE 149
OUR SYNTHETIC WORLD 152
THE WISDOM OF SATAN 154
EUPHONY 155
CELESTIAL NAVIGATION 156
SHANGHAI WAIF 157
GOOD OLD WORLD! 161
THE THOROUGHBRED 163
BEAUTY AND THE BEAST 165
MANY HAPPY RETURNS 166
ALIBI JULIUS E. 169
OLD BILL 170
AN APPRECIATION OF NOTHING 171
THANK GOD. FOR THAY 172
WHY NOT? 173
BRUTUS WAS AN HONORABLE MAN! 174
THIS REVOLVING WORLD 175
AN HOUR 176
DESERT DREAMS 178
FORBIDDEN FRUIT 181
THE GREAT WALL OF CHINA 185
THE STORY TELLER 186
MANCHURIA 187
THE PASSING OF OLD LANDMARKS 193
WINE OF HUMAN KINDNESS 197

CONTENTS

PLEASE COME AGAIN   198
ODE TO LADY BOUNTIFUL   199
RAINBOW CHASERS   203
IN DEFENSE OF NONSENSE   206
THE FORGOTTEN MAN   208
THE FORGOTTEN WOMAN   209
A BEACHCOMBER'S LAMENT   211
MAGNIFICENCE OF FAILURE   212
RESOLUTIONS   214
THE SWAN-SONG OF A REFUGEE   216
WHEN WE GO SAILING HOME   218
THE JOLLY STEWARD   223
STOP! LOOK! LOOSEN!   224
LAZY DAYS   225
MAN OVERBOARD   226
CHIMES O'THE SEA   227
TALES O'THE SEA   228
A WHALE OF A JONAH   229
OHIO DE GOZAIMASU! IRASHAI!   230
AS WE SEE OTHERS   231
OLD CAP SAYS!   233
THE FAIR PACIFIC   234
FATHER NEPTUNE   235
THE WAYSIDE ISLES   238
ISLES OF LIQUID SUNSHINE   239
FAREWELL TO OUR STEAMER   241
THE CAPTAIN'S BALL   242
LAND AHOY!   243
HOME AGAIN   244
THE LURE OF THE EAST   245

Glossary

"A"

AMAH

Bachelor's housekeeper — Cook amah
Children's nurse — Young master amah —
 Young missie amah
House maid — House amah
Ladies' maid — Missie amah
Laundress — Wash amah
Waitress — Table amah

AQUA VITAE

Distilled spirits for the stilled spirits.

"B"

BANYAN TREE

A tree which grows with its roots in the
air — according to the guide books.

BELONG PLOPPER

Etiquette

BIRTHDAY

An excuse to get tight.

BLOATED BROKER

One who makes money out of our losses.

BLOOMING LIZARDS

Equivalent of pink elephants.

BLUE DEVILS

Equivalent of pink elephants.

BOY

> The satanic friend, guide, philosopher and
> wet nurse to foreigners in the Far East.
> Bath boy —
> Hotel porter —
> Room boy —
> Waiter.

BUM BOAT MAN

> A river or harbour hawker who sells any-
> thing at exorbitant prices to jackies.

BUND

> Water front

"C"

CATHAY

> Ancient and romantic name for China,
> now used mostly by stay-at-home writ-
> ers.

CHITS

> Personal currency in the form of magic
> slips of paper which bring more joy than
> Aladdin's lamp — until the day of judg-
> ment when the schroff or bill collector is
> on hand at the very moment the signer's
> pay is due.

CHIN CHIN

> Greetings! Good fortune! Astonishing
> luck!

CHOP CHOP
Makee hurry!
CLOCK TALKEE PLOPPER FACE
Keeping correct time.
COMPRADORE
A friend of the needy clerk.
A cashier plus.
An expert money changer who guaratees
to keep the proprietor free from loss
through bad credit or bad currency — in
exchange for a small salary and the
privilege of handling the firm's or indi-
vidual's money to conduct a private loan
business — at exorbitant interest. This
latter phase of his activities is something
which does not concern the proprietor.
CONSULS
Nurse maids for tourists.

"D"

DAMN
Shamus' pet expression — It doesn't mean a
damn thing
DAN DAN IKA DUI
(Presto change) — Hokus Pokus
DEACON
A rare species in the Far Eastern ports.

DRAM
 A drink of liquor that is too small for a he
 man.
DUI **D**AN **D**AN
 (Presto change) — Hokus Pokus

"E"

THE **E**AST
 Places East of Suez where the
 commonplace is strange. Where a man
 can have a debit before he knows he has
 it. Where angels are rare and men are
 glad of it.

"F"

FACE
 As precious to a man as a maiden's honor
 to her mother. An intangible attribute of
 men, families and firms in the Far East —
 native or foreign — which must be saved
 at all costs.
FILTHY **LUCRE**
 Something no gentleman should touch —
FLOWER **B**OATS
 The floating equivalent of a private caba-
 ret.
FOPPISH **N**ABOB
 Big butter-and-egg man.

"G"

GRIFFIN
> Young horse which is racing its first
> year—also applied to a young man in his
> first year out in the East.

GOB
> British sailor's equivalent of Limey.

GUZABOS
> Dictionarians are now working on this—
> Guys who know all about something.

"H"

HELL
> Shamus' pet express number two.

HEL-UV-A
> Latin-term of endearment.

HONG
> Place of business of one eligible for
> admittance to the Club.
> Where signs are taken in at night.
> Where an advertisement is called an
> announcement.
> Where things can be sold in small
> quantities only if they are called
> samples.

HONGKONGESE
> Descendants of modern Marco Polos.

HONGKONG
    Hongkong is an island in the Southern
    China Sea.
    A colony as British as a British Isle can be.
    The safest of all havens to be found in
    seven seas.
    For ex-official patriots and Chinese
    refugees.

HOTELS
    — Where West meets East.

HUNYADI JANOS
    A Hungarian mineral water which is
    noted for its dynamic effect.

"I"
IGA-LANG-TANG
    Name of famous Peking magician.
IKA DUI DAN DAN
    (Presto change) — Hokus Pokus
INNOCENTS
    Those who have not been burned by fire
    before leaving home.

"J"
JOSS
    Heaven business — Luck —
    Bad joss — Bad luck
    Good joss — Good luck

JUNK
> A boat which is too big to be a sampan.

"K"

KUBLA KHAN
> The Emperor who gave Marco Polo four-
> teen wives.

KOWTOW
> The Chinese equivalent of "turning
> the other cheek" — (No belong today
> fashion.)

"L"

LASCAR
> East Indian native sailor with
> salamandarine qualities.

LICHII
> A cross between a fruit and a nut. Much
> over-rated.

LIMEY
> American sailor's equivalent of Gob.

LURE OF THE EAST
> A drug

"M"

MANGO
> A much over-rated tropical fruit.

MANGOSTEEN
> A much over-rated tropical fruit.

MASKEE
>Go as far as you like—
>Have it your own way—
>I don't care—
>It makes no difference—
>It can't be helped—
>It matters not—
>It's all right with me-
>It's O.K. with me—
>Let the other fellow worry—
>Why should I worry?

MONOCLE
>A single lens which prevents its wearer
>from seeing more at one time than his
>mind can comprehend.

"N"

NABOB
>One who mistakes money, or rank, for
>quality.

NUMBER ONE
>Topside Boss
>Number one boy (See Boy)

"P"

PACIFIC, The fair
>A damn lie

PADDLE BOATS OF HUMAN POWER
>Junks operated by a paddle wheel which
>is revolved by a number of coolies on a

tread-mill — in exchange for their passage.

Sometimes called rice-power boats.

PEAK

Hongkongites heaven

PIPING CROAKERS

Antithesis of bloated brokers.

P.P.C.'s

Pour prendre congé — to take leave. Cards mailed by ordinary humans but inserted in the local newspaper by the blasé bonton.

"R"

RAJAH

An occidental conception of an oriental potentate.

A'RABBITT

"Almost unbelievably, not a pen name." — (Japan Chronicle)

"S"

SHAMUS

Handle to A'Rabbitt's name.

SAVVY

Perspicacity.

SAP

The forgotten man —
The meek shall inherit the earth after the aggressive have taken possession of

Heaven. (S.A'R.)

SAMPAN

Any small boat in the Far East.

SHAMEEN

The foreign settlement in Canton.

SHROFF

Compradore's handy man — collector.

SIKHS

Religious policemen.

SING SONG MAIDEN

Professional singing girl, to amuse the tired business man.

SNOB

A plumber East of the Suez —

One who has an instinctive feeling that he does not merit his social position and is therefore afraid to know anyone of lesser rank — or, one who has been thoroughly snubbed in the course of his social climbing and instinctively passes it on to others whom he believes to be beneath him on the social ladder.

S-P-C-A

Society for the perpetuation of canine activities.

SWEEPSTAKES

Where "many are called" to buy tickets and "few are chosen" to receive prizes. A sweepstake may be held on the outcome of a horse race, a marriage or what-not.

"T"

TAIPAN

Big boss —

Number one gink who monopolizes the
head of the bar at the club and frowns on
young clerks, or "clarks".

TEMPLE OF LO HAN

Temple of the five hundred genii in Can-
ton where there is a statue of Marco
Polo — with 499 others gods for worship.

TIFFIN

A mid-day meal of such proportions as to
induce sleep.

TYPHOON

Big wind.

"V"

VOLSTEAD — A misguided American.

"W"

WANCHEE

The first law of nature.

WORTHY HOAX

A charitable affair at which 90 per cent of
the funds are spent to amuse the philan-
thropists.

"Y"

YANKEE

Every other American except me —

BALLADS OF THE EAST

by

SHAMUS A'RABBITT

Illustrations by "Sapajou"

SHANGHAI
1937

Prologue

I've lived a life of travel,
In many foreign lands;
I've met rovers of all nations,
With hearts cleaner than their hands.

I've found them most like children
Who love to play and sing —
To pulsate with the Heavens,
And with every living thing.

My simple rhymes and ballads
Were made for men like these,
Who love the Love and Friendship
Of the rovers overseas.

SHAMUS A'RABBITT

3

SHAMUS A'RABBITT

The Lure of the East

O, what is the call
That comes to us all
When once we have been in the EAST —
To lure us away
For life and a day
In tropics to rot in the EAST.

Away from our fields —
Where no harvest yields
A fragrance on which we may FEAST —
No walks in the woods
With trees and their moods
No orchards to bloom in the EAST —

No strolls by the streams
Where tropic sun gleams
No skylarks to sing in the EAST —
No welcome within
A countryside inn
Not out in old Asia at LEAST!

We roam o'er the lands
With sweat on our hands
Discomfort for man and for BEAST —
The mildew's a fright
On boots overnight
'Tis muggy and damp in the EAST —

Where roaches eat books
And lizards from nooks
Will sport on our walls in the EAST—
Where snakes and the ants
Will sleep in our pants
And flies on our food make a FEAST—

It rains and it rains
Till blocking our drains
For sewers we've none in the EAST—
There's a "symphony" of smell
No language can tell
But yet we return to the EAST—

To filth we are blind
Benumbed is the mind
But still we go back to the EAST—
We call in at Cook's
And are happy he books
To where LOVE—is
    the love of the
        EAST!

Marco Polo

Young Marco Polo, sturdy man,
Took walks that you and I
Might think of but we hardly can
Complete before we die.

He took a stroll, ten thousand miles,
And left his wife at home;
To win the sing-song maiden's smiles,
Half round the world from Rome.

'Tis said, the longest way he took—
Where naught but camels go;
O'er desert, hills, through stream and brook
And Himalaya's snow.

When he arrived in Far Cathay,
This husky drew a prize;
For Kubla Khan that very day,
Bestowed him fourteen wives.

And so in history it is said,
A place at court had he;
For thirty years betimes he strayed
Along the China Sea.

Till finally he longed for change,
And homeward set his course;
To leave those days one could arrange
Without e'en a divorce.

But Kubla was a crafty bird,
Whose life was full of spice.
From Marco's wives the plan he heard
And smote him in a trice!

When Marco sent his P. P. C.'s
And chits to friends in town;
Prepared to sail off on the seas—
Then Kubla's trap was thrown.

So Marco tarried for a spell,
A tough old dog was he;
And soon again he worked like—well,
He then slipped off to sea!

He sailed the China Coast one day
And left his wives to cry;
And tacked around by Indi-a,
Without e'en a "Good Bye!"

7

Old Kubla tried to imitate
The ships that Marco built—
Constructed with his wealth of state,
A fleet "armed to the hilt!"

But Marco made his 'get-away'.
With loot that filled his trunks;
Left Kubla's ships until this day,
A fine old fleet of junks:

Still sailing on the China Coast,
With cannons at the rail;
They're not for looks of much to boast,
Gadzooks, but they can sail!

Built on the lines Columbus drew—
When he cribbed old Marco's plans;
And followed Marco's travels too,
But struck uncharted lands.

And thus, we see, 'twas Marco who
Reversed the roads to Rome;
And paved the way for me — and you,
To get away from Home.

Now China honors Marco's name,
In temple of Lo Han;
With bronzed "five hundred Gods of Fame,"
He sits in old Canton.

The Call Of The East

To the uninitiated
This tale is here related,
In the East—Ye Griffins listen one and all:
It is a point of etiquette
Our BOYS have never broken yet,
Of obeying but the Masters—of the CALL.

"Oh, Boy, bring me this
And Boy, bring me that,
And Boy, bring me everything
Including Master's hat!"

It is not Buoy nor Boi—
But more like "Ship ahoy!"
Commanding like Napoleon, strong
    and proud:
'Tis not the act of shouting hoarse
But comes to those in time of course,
Who will Live and pay the Piper if allowed!

"Oh, Boy bring the towel
And Boy, bring the soap,
And Boy, you can rub me down—
Without you there's no hope!"

* * * * * * *

The Boy is here my saviour as
I'm such a haughty thing;
At Home perhaps a plumber but
Out in the East a King!
When I go up to Heaven and
If Peter frowns on me,
I'm sure my voice will greet him with—
"Oh, Boy, bring the KEY!"

Maskee!

If gains or losses be our lot
"Maskee" is what we sing!
The East's the place to worry not—
'Tis maskee everything!

I cabled to the other side
And this is what I got:
My call was for my promised bride;
Maskee, she loved me not!

I married me another girl—
An idol of the East;
And swimmingly we're in the whirl,
Maskee, come join the feast!

I sign more chits within a month
Than I can ever pay;
But everyone here knows the stunt—
Maskee, not here to stay!

Of course there are the honest men
Who spend their lives to save;
And lose all in a minute—then—
Maskee, a tidal wave!

I held the number for the Sweep
They called me "Lucky Sinner!"
I stood the Club champagne — 'twas cheap —
Maskee, I'd drawn a winner!

Then "Wifey" purchased diamond rings
And gowns begay resplendent;
I'm sailing on my credit's wings —
Maskee, I'm independent!

But oh, alas, I must relate,
It is the Truth that shocks!
The number was but a mistake
Maskee, I'm on the rocks!

If gains or losses be our lot
"Maskee" is what we sing!
The East's the place to worry not,
'Tis maskee everything!

Though honest
Or dishonest
'Tis the same thing
In the end:
There'll always be
The spenders where
The Compradore
Will lend.

Snub, Snobs and Snobbery

'Tis a wise man
Who knows he's a snob,
And a fool
Who shows it!

*　　*　　*　　*　　*　　*　　*

O, a sudden change of fortune
Is awful as a rule;
For it makes a decent fellow
Act like a bally fool!

If it's down then he'll go crazy,
If up he'll lose his job;
He becomes so tired and lazy
Or, worst of all, a snob!

It is not a case of merit
In strata like our soil;
'Tis the air that we inherit
Or comes if we strike "oil".

Then we have our social earthquakes,
Landslides or tidal wave—
And will not enjoy our handshakes
Where snobs will misbehave.

* * * * * * *

When I drifted to the Orient,
I knew not what I'd find;
But of work I had some fair intent
And started in to grind.

It was then I met the Taipan
And dazzled by his *crown*;
With the Griffins joined in *worshipping*
These *worthies* of renown:

"Come plebes and loudly sing, Rejoice—let
praises ring—
(If not you'll ne'er get on)
Come join our loving song!
          (sotto) *All is well!*"

"Taipans omnipotent,
Ye gods of the Orient —
O, deign to look at us
Thou great and *virtuous!*
       (sotto) *Go to H-ll!*"

And years later did these Griffins
Become great Taipans too;
Now each day before their tiffins
They stand as Taipans do:

With our Royalty while drinking
Their cocktails at the Club;
And have joined the worthies thinking Young
Griffins they should snub.

      * * * * * * *

Oh, the small fleas they have others
To bite them or applaud;
And 'tis thus the world's revolving
With many overawed!

There is Mrs. Big-Bank-Jones
And Mrs. Small-Bank-Smith:
Mrs. Outside-Customs owns
Mrs. Inside's "It!"

'Tis hard to be "unsnobbish"
When guests make such a noise;
While they're sipping tea from saucers
To horrify our "boys";

Or, when peas fall from the knife-blade
To soil our nice new rugs—
When the home-brew that "the wife" made
Is served to us in mugs!

Then there is the snob of motors
Who'll think he is a LORD;
Just because his name-plate-letters
Do not happen to spell FORD.

Or, the snob who's always talking
Of other fellow's rank;
When we know d--n well he's waiting
The day when he can swank!

But of all the snobs the biggest—
Who'll try to make a hit;
By a-butting where unwelcome
And snubbed he gets for it!

Now with all our worldly wisdom,
Philosophy and such;
We can't fill the world with reason
Nor riddles answer much:

But I've written of our "snobbers"
Till truth has been disclosed;
That we know the men who snub us
Are but ourselves exposed;

With the snubbed ones and the others
Who flayed the snobs and tried;
Make men think they're not all brothers—
We know that they have lied!

* * * * * * *

To make a man a snob
He must be snubbed.
He won't get snubbed
Who stays where he belongs.
No man with pride will go
Where he'll get rubbed,
And so will ne'er blame others
For his wrongs.

18

Hongkong Jazz

O, why do we go to the Hongkong Grill,
O, why do we go to the Lounge?
And why do we wrinkle our brow at the bill,
And why do we dance to the sounds

Of saxophone, kettle and flute—
That wrigglum riddlum wiggly bazz
With shake of a shimmy
And blare of a jazz?

O, why do we motor to Repulse Bay,
O, why do we stay in the swim?
O, why do we curse and look back at the day
We learned how to dance with a vim

To saxophone, kettle and flute —
That wrigglum riddlum wiggly bazz
With shake of a shimmy
And blare of a jazz?

O, many's the year that we saved our rocks,
To build us a home in old age!
And purchased the best of the bonds and
the stocks
Before the old jazz was the rage —

With saxophone, kettle and flute —
That wrigglum riddlum wiggly bazz
The shake of a shimmy
And blare of a jazz?

O, why do I sing such a doleful tale
Of one who was owner of stocks?
Because I'm reduced to old kippers and ale —
The jazz it put me on the rocks!

Changez Vous Dames

"Jack Sprat could eat no fat —
His wife could eat no lean."

A six foot boy should worry if
A girl of bare fourteen
(And plus ten) measures up
To five foot one at least
For fox trot and the one-step at
Our evening dancing feast.
And if a maiden six feet two
Should hop around the floor —
Perhaps she finds amusement if
Her partner's five feet four.

Shadows

J. Stickem MacWithers, a Singapore lad,
A froliesome begot though not very bad —
With a gay bachelor's wealth and renown,
His parties were often the talk of the town.

Till one day, surprising, he brought out a
     bride,
Without e'en advising his "boys" on the side;
So when Mac vacated his home the next day,
For club duly slated the usual way —

His "boy" was much worried by what was in
     bed,
And finally entered the room and there said:
"Much sorry missie — what thing makee slow?
My Master no likee — when missie no go!"

Honesty

Ah Tack he cooked as cooks will do
For Engineers, and good ones too;
The lads were Scotch and did not like
The way their wine would fade from sight.

They called the Boy and "Hop" said they:
"How fashion him sherry make get-away?"
"Me no can savvy you talkee him cook!"
Hop gave the lads an innocent look.

The sherry decanter was filled that night
With Hunyadi Janos corked in tight;
Next day 'twas gone the usual way,
They called the Cook, he heard them say:

"What fashion you take him sherry, you snoop?"
Ah Tack just grinned: "For Master's soup!"

EXIT COOK!

23

The Jewel

A slave could not attend a queen,
E'en though attached for life;
As faithfully as did Ah Chien
Who served my little wife.

"Oh, hubby dear, 'tis wonderful,
Ah Chien is so discreet;
He never comes within my room
Until I'm dressed complete!"

"That's good Ah Chien (said I) you're trained.
I wonder how you tell,
That Missie's finished dressing;
You seem to know so well!"

Ah Chien replied: "Him Number One,
B'long plopper talkee me;
No come when Missie no have clothes —
More better lookee key-hole see!"

24

One Head and a Double Thought

The Smiths and Browns lived side by side
Both men and wives became good friends —
Their servant problems they'd confide —
What did they learn? Well, that depends!

'Twas oft' they found comparing notes,
That what one left the other got;
If one had chaff, the other oats,
At one meal cold the next meal hot.

They joined their forces one fine day.
Agreed — they jointly took a look —
Within their kitchens twain, and say I
They found there but a single cook!

SHAMUS A'RABBITT

Passion in the Kitchen

Our boy stood on the burning deck,
Committed he a crime;
He kissed the Amah on the neck,
Quite out of place and time.

The Missie said: "What ho! You there!
That was a beastly trick;
Apologize, and too beware!
You'd better do it quick!"

Our Boy stands on the burnt out deck,
He's sorry for his crime;
For when he gazed on Amah's neck,
He kissed the second time.

Celestial Vintage

Sir Alex Roserio dined in great style.
Befitting a worthy old sport;
With service the talk for many a mile,
And wines of the very best sort.

Inviting the Deacon to dine he attempted,
To coach his old "boy" in the art;
Of serving a dinner where wines are exempted,
For guests with a blue-ribbon heart.

Sir Alex gave warning as "Boy" was progressing,
In serving the soup at the dinner;
Aside he had whispered: "Oh, wait Boy, the blessing!"
And twinkled his eye — the — ol' sinner.

Inscrutable poise in no whit diminished,
The "Boy" told the Master with grief:
"B'long vely sorry, that bottle have finished"
And shocked the grave Deacon's belief.

The Paymaster

Our Padre took his walk one day,
Upon our after deck;
Resembled he our 'old dog Pay',
And soon around his neck;

Two lovely arms flung from behind—
The Chinese Flower Girl,
Mistook for Pay, the Padre kind,
And soon these words she hurled:

"Oh, Master Master, velly bad Joss,
Me kiss him Heaven Man;
Number-one-top-side-Christian God.
Excuse me, one time can!"

HOW

These are the days of the HOW books
How to do this or that —
How to improve our fading looks
How to make father grow fat —
How to bring up the baby or
How to grow forests of hair —
How to love the ladies or
How to make money from air —
How to concoct a short story by
Men who have not written one —
How to grow old before we die —
How to mix labor with fun —
But the beggar that gets me I'll confess —
The bird who ought to be jailed —
Is the guy who wrote a book on success
And then — by heavens — he FAILED!

East and West

The East and West make many a jest,
O'er laws of opposites;
Where we have strife, their peaceful life
Is Hell on Western wits.

Whereas we dash and sometimes crash—
Activity they hate—
They push, we pull: they're masterful,
As passively they wait.

For ages past they've been outclassed,
For speed and comfort too;
But times have changed and now, though strange,
They're building as we do.

For Western things, their anvil rings—
Their mills are grinding too—
At times think we that Industry
Will yet unite these two.

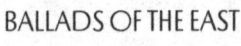

Chinese Joss

A tourist thought
    a quip he'd toss —
He asked how the
    dead behave!

"Oh, hello Cheng,
    what thing this joss —
Samshu before the grave?
When do the spirits
    drink their wine?
Oh, what are the festive hours?"

Friend Cheng replied: "Oh, velly fine —
All same your dead man smelly flowers!"

The Minute Man in Shanghai

While strolling down the Bund one day,
Before the stroke of noon;
I saw a gunner cross the way —
The Time we'd all know soon.

He stopped to light his cigarette,
And casu-ally play;
And speak to everyone he met —
Then bang! 'Twas noon of day!

Approaching jovial John I said:
"How savvy you pull string?"
He answered, "Me have got one head,
Him velly easy thing!"

"My flen Sing Fat one clock have got,
Him talkee plopper face;
And evly day him savvy what,
I lookee Sing Fat's place!"

Next day when passing Sing Fat's shop,
    I thought I'd take a look:
I asked him if his clock "make stop,"
    How plopper time he took?

Said he: "On Bund side got one gun,
    And evly day at noon;
When twelve o'clock he make blum blum!
    I fixee him clock soon."

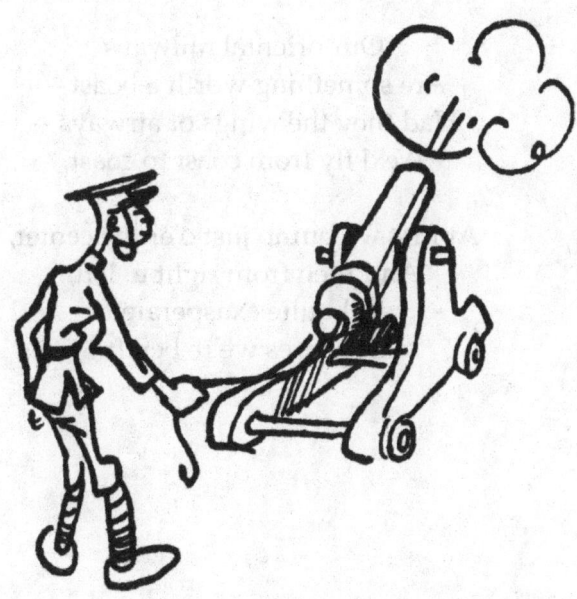

The Devil's Railways

Our oriental railways
Are something worth a boast—
Had they the wings of airways—
We'd fly from coast to coast.

At first we bump just o'er the center,
And then from right to left;
Till quite exasperated
Of senses we're bereft.

There's nothing more that we can say
But duly recommend;
The Devil he should travel on
These lines from end to end.

In cars quite well selected and
With nicely flattened wheels;
So every time they'd go around,
They'd bump upon the steels.

And after that if he survives,
With health and mind still sound;
He'll go to Hell for comfort and
Will make the wheels all round.

Iga Lang Tang

(The Chinese Magician)

>"Iga lang tang
>Ika dui dan dan
>Dan dan ika dui
>Dui dan dan!"

Came through the dust of old Pekin
This chant above the plagued din
Of swarthy men with palanquin
And slant-eyed maiden fares within.

>"Iga lang tang
>Ika dui dan dan
>Dan dan ika dui
>Dui dan dan!"

Again it came above the crowd
With intonations clear and loud
A wonder-man performed—kowtowed
Produced a rabbit—once more bowed:

>"Iga lang tang
>Ika dui dan dan
>Dan Dan ika dui
>Dui Dan dan!"

While deft of hand each magic word
Brought forth a gold-fish or a bird
From hats or places quite absurd —
We marvelled as we gaped and heard:

> "Iga lang tang
> Ika dui dan dan
> Dan dan ika dui
> Dui dan dan!"

Three peas upon a stand we saw
Three walnut shells without a flaw
To hide the peas till we with awe
Beheld a pigeon — peas in claw:

> "Iga lang tang
> Ika dui dan dan
> Dan dan ika dui
> Dui dan dan!"

"Ten cents please!"

The Henpecked Husbands of Chikiang

The hen-pecked husbands of Chikiang
All met one day in conclave brave —
By their ancestors in the grave!
They swore that they would all enslave
Their absent wives and misbehave —
The nagging wives of Chikiang.

Then lo, behold, from Chikiang!
The wives soon came as they had heard —
(The crows had echoed every word —)
With kitchen implements absurd
Each cackling like an angry bird
To flay the men of Chikiang.

They chased these braves of Chikiang
Who ran like rabbits wild, 'tis said;
These brave bold men distraught dismayed
Took to the hills lest they get flayed —
Only one poor man behind had stayed —
Defying the wives of Chikiang.

When the men returned to Chikiang
They thought that it would be quite meet
To reward the man who held his seat —
To make him hero of the street —
They found him seated white as a sheet
Stark dead from fright in Chikiang.

SHAMUS A'RABBITT

Rain, Rain, Beautiful Rain!

With the heat at ninety-seven,
And the moisture ninety-two;
Hongkong is like a — (heaven)
With its cloud-bursts and its dew.

With the rancid perspiration
On our nicely laundered clothes,
When we try in desperation
To evade the season's blows!

By wetting down our "innerds"
Through the fear they might go dry;
Till we see the "blooming lizards"
And we ask the Doctor why!

When our gloomy drooping spirits
Ever long for sun to shine,
And blue devils make us fear it's
For the spirits we repine.

Through the torrents mixed with drizzle,
When there's naught to do but drip;
Through the ninety-seven sizzle,
When we never miss a sip.

We may have our "housing problem"
And pay cash for every drink,
While the landlord's tenants *rob* 'em
And the legislators wink.

Where the air is full of romance,
Of "ye olden days," they tell;
When the real estate was no man's
And the business boomed "like hell"!

When the daily occupation
In the ever-luring East,
Was to watch the stock-inflation —
'Tis the tale they tell, at least!

How we feel like "piping croakers",
With our business "gone to pot";
And are all — but bloated brokers —
Here a-dying of the rot.

Yes, a-dying but not drying
In the ever-rotting mould;
Through the torrid summer crying
For our dirty pot of gold.

Through the heat and damp repining,
Through the rainy season's rains;
Since the sun has stopped his shining,
We have mildew on our brains.

It's apparent in this rhyming,
And with every rotten pun,
While the rain outside is chiming;
"Oh, there never was a Sun!"

Progress

Up to seven mother's darling,
After seven Sunday school—
Up to twenty looking forward,
After twenty play the fool.

Up to thirty acts regretful,
After thirty think again—
Up to forty seeking pleasure,
After forty dodging pain.

Up to fifty slipping backward,
After fifty sad and sore—
Up to sixty drooping sadly,
After sixty, pay the score.

A Man of Clay

When I was a boy I had a great fear
That I'd be a grump by my fiftieth year.

To school — then I married a charming young wife
And like a good citizen settled for life —

Till swollen with pride and self-righteous conceit
I worked out a creed for "the man in the street."

A wicked young sinner who called himself friend
Induced me one time to bespend a week-end —

In hills where we played at an out-of-door game
Which captured my Sundays and killed my good
        name —

A game made for youngsters, old dufferes and nuts
To drive a wee ball o'er a field full of ruts —

Rewards for the game I'll confess there were none
    Just drive and then finding the ball and I won.

But now — like the story — to make a tale short —
I'm near middle age and a lover of sport —

A lover of home and a lover of friends —
What I think of "World Beaters" — that all depends!

Old colleagues they think me a man made of clay
Of them what I think — it is just by the way:

With highly arched brows o'er their heavy-rimmed
    glasses
They say that I'm clay but I think they are asses.

Watch Your Step

Step up please!
Step down—be careful!
This way to the right—
That way to the left!
Step lively!
Watch your step!

Keep off the grass!
Positively no admittance!
No smoking allowed!
Dogs or children not wanted!
Step lively!
Watch your step!

Don't say that—
'Tis not the thing!
Don't wear that—'tis passe'!
You must not mix with those people—
But you must call on Mrs. So and So!
Step lively!
Watch your step!

Don't eat that!
Don't drink this—not now!
You mustn't go there!—
Till half past five.
Step lively!

So this is LIFE!
Thank you Doctor,
Make mine chloroform!

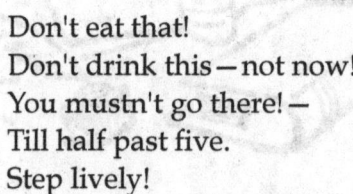

Virtue Rewarded

I dreamt a night or two ago,
I made a trip to Hell
And what I saw surprised me so,
Perhaps I'd better tell!

At first I called at Dante's place,
To ask about the rent.
I thought that he would know of space
In that establishment.

He showed rotiseries where
They mixed the fat and lean.
Where sizzling somewhat filled the air
But still 'twas Dev'lish clean.

I saw the inmates turned about
Revolved each on a spike;
I saw them roasted inside-out
In ways I would not like.

But I was soon surprised to see
Where devils blew off smoke;
Were roasting birds quite full of glee
Who took it as a joke.

I asked Old Dan' just what this meant—
The smiles on those now toasted—
He said: "They're Consuls now content,
They're used to being 'roasted'."

White Nights

O, would that God
The giftie gie us
To see sea-serpents
As they see us!

(Apologies to a good cigar)

* * * * * * * * * * * *

Our birthdays come but once a year—
For celebrating—far or near—
Hongkong's the best of places—
We sail around Elusive Bay
Where mermaidens come by day
To sun their pretty faces.

And when the evening sunset glow
Enflames the sea all yachtsmen know
'Tis balm for worldly troubles—
When flickering birthday-candle-light
Casts grotesque shadows on the night
We taste the wine that bubbles.

On chow to bring a rajah glee
With mango mangosteen lichi
We dine in peace and plenty—
And just for luck a dram or two
What else can Royal Yachtsmen do
Who've passed the age of twenty?

What more to top a merry spree
For lusty sailors on the sea
Who dine and wine like youngsters—
Than to carouse until sunrise
Athwart the rail to look in eyes
Of wriggling squirming monsters—

To see a writhing slimy snake
And count the bubbles in his wake
With glee describe his features—
To note the labels on his back
Of our pet brands—Alas, alack!
DRYLAND has no such creatures.

Dusky but True

O, yes, she is dusky but true to me!
Ungraceful but trusty — no blue eyes to see.

Yes, coarse are her tresses — all that do I know —
Her waddle distresses me when we're on show!

And though we're not married —
    yet, always it grieves her
When down town I've tarried and
    home I must leave her.

She waits at the landing a light in
    her eyes —
And never demanding excuses nor
    lies.

Yes, oft have I wondered just
    how I should fare
Instead were I greeted by maid of
    fair hair!

But beggars like me who've been long in the jungle
Are awkward with maidens — their ways will we bungle.

In truth would I rather face lions like Daniel
Than wed a fair maiden and give up my Spaniel.

51

SHAMUS A'RABBITT

The Canton River

From snowy mantle — season's change —
Released from Himalaya's Range —
This turbid teeming river flows —
Ne'er more resembling mountain snows.

Down where it meets the inward tide
It bears the busy boats that glide
On ebb and flow from East to West
And West to East upon their quest.

The ceaseless moving slipper boats
And every craft that sails or floats
Provide the homes for families more
Than ever will set foot on shore.

The ferry-man e'er leads the clan
With daughter crying — "take sampan!"
The hawkers shout what they can do
To make a suit or mend a shoe.

The floating barbers shave, shampoo —
And then adorn the heads anew
Of butchers, bakers, fishermen too;
'Tis hard to tell what they won't do.

They come and go and swiftly glide
So fascinating on the tide

With many ages at the oars —
A swarming mass — life out-of-doors —

With children fast lest they should fall
From over sides beyond their call —
Like a knap-sack or a monkish hood
To some are strapped a float of wood.

A husky healthy tribe are they
From singing rowing every day —
When traffic fails to clear the way
The old and young will swear and bray:

They'll shower curses rich with doom
To shatter each ancestral tomb —
And pull to give each other room
From sweeping oar and swinging boom.

And, from the dawn to night they'll swarm
Through heat of day till evening warm
When each boat finds its resting place
Somewhere upon the river's face.

They may be seen as one by one
They pull for shore — the day's work done —
And soon the smoking incense fine
Resmoulders on the family shrine.

Before the shades of evening steal
Aromas of the family meal —
Then comes the pipe and evening glow
While phantom junks e'er come and go:

Emerging silently with awe —
With woven sails of golden straw —
They pass in dusky shadows by
Like phantoms cross the Western sky.

And oft from Neptune's caverns creep
With boatmen step by step to keep
The treadmills going by the hour
Come paddle boats of human power.

Returning too are Delta Junks —
Built high of cabins filled with bunks —
With sides a gaily painted mass
Of colored dragons — devil class;

They come and go with sweep and sail —
Past flower-boats that never fail
To distract our reverie
With raucous sounds of revelry:

With sounds of cymbals, drums and gongs
The foppish nabobs sing their songs
These flower boats of gilt and glass
Are symbols of the ruling class.

Adown among the anchored boats
The bumboat man forever floats —
In unison his sweep and cry —
He sells concoctions — wet and dry —

And as the shades of night e'er creep
O'er darkening waters — some may sleep —
Whilst others wake to ply their trade —
As carried on since world was made.

Like cockles bobbing up and down
The night-life swarms this water town —
From birth to death each tragic page
Of Life is written on its age:

For centuries centuries on end we're told —
These river folk both young and old —
Have plied these waters with their song —
Whilst dynasties have come and gone.

＊ ＊ ＊ ＊ ＊ ＊ ＊

From North and South and East and West
Incessant o'er the Delta's breast —
This river bears its burden down
In sorrow passing through our town
A symbol of the heaven's tears —
Flows placidly — ten thousand years!

SHAMUS A'RABBITT

Humane Society Ball

Oh, they came from near and far
In their rickshaw, chair or car
To do honor to the S.P.C.A. Ball.
They were hauled by strong and weak
Shouldered up and down the Peak
But they looked aristo-cratic one and all.

There Sir John, and then, Sir David
With their ladies fair though aged
And our men each with his gayest de-co-ra-tion
Then our ladies some be-ermined
As they turned out quite determined
To be masters of the newest syn-co-pa-tion.

I speak not with asperity
They were out again for charity
And sincerely they were doing what they should.
So they show their generosity
In this ball for aristocracy
And by turning out for every cause that's good.

Oh, without them our small island
Would be left without a smile — and
As a nation we'd be hardly worth a damn.
They're the raisins in the pudding
That'll swell when in the cooking —
As essential as the bone is to the ham.

And as they all assembled
These knights-of-old resembled
Ancient History: — when the music struck the air.
The dancers tripped around the floor
In rhythmic time with Terpsichore
'Twas exciting for the dames who came to stare.

There were two of these I overheard
And to you may I tell every word
Quite truthful as a sober scribe should do?
They loved the darling dogs and cats
And talked of cruel-ty to rats
And of habits of the Natives — much ado!

Friend to friend replied: "They're awful
Oh, I mean the Natives, so unlawful
'Twas tonight my husband thrashed one on the way.
Oh, they swarm like flies around one
The beasts: — you know about them,
With such loads they block our streets near every day — "

It was time that I should hear no more
Then sad and weary and foot-sore
I betook me to my room to write this log
To sing praises of this wor-thy hoax —
"The more I see of some folks"
As the poets say: "The more I like my dog."

The Typhoon

O batter my windows — blow and blow —
Ye winds from over the seas!
Tonight I'm snug — where'er ye go —
Ensconced at home with Ease.

But when ye shake and rattle the pane
And tear at my roof and door
And bring to your aid my old friend rain
I know that we've met before.

Last year when ye tore my sails away
And left me to wallow the sea
Ye gave me the thrill I feel today —
To stir up the soul in me —

But where O vagrant have ye been
Through all the seasons round?
What have ye shattered and torn since then?
What ships have ye cast aground?

And why do I love your fiery teeth
That hiss and spit in the gale?
Is it because my soul ye greet
With something that will not quail?

Something that's left of primitive man
That's handed down to me?
Something of battle which never can
From brute in man be free?

Why do ye rise and fall and lash and flay
And shake and writhe and roll?
Why more ugly at night than day
And why do ye take such toll?

Perchance you're akin to man and beast
From North and South and West —
And others who sing when ye come from
    the East
The songs from deep in the breast!

Songs that we sing but when ye blow
Songs that are wild and free —
Songs of a life lived long ago —
Songs for a Man o' the Sea!

The King O'Shameen

Sir Jimminy J, a king by the way,
Who rules o'er the land o'Shameen;
A small piece of sand the size of your hand,
An island o'ercovered with green:

Where doves bill and coo with maidens to
    woo
For marriage by Jimminy J;
O'er avenues green the banyan trees lean,
E'er cooling the tropical day.

Sir Jim he holds court, the jolly old sport,
And savage is he to the sinner;
But whene'er he dines and samples our wines
Sir J is the life of the dinner.

Sir J takes a fling—Judge, Consul and King—
At times he will threaten demonical;
To give bread and water, or hang, draw and
    quarter
All those within range of his monocle.

Sir Jim he has neighbors who rattle their
    sabres,
But with regal regalia re-gina;
He soothes all the natives with his palliatives
In the neighboring province of China.

And so it is clear there's never a fear,
Wherever our flag may be seen;
Our consuls hold sway like Jimminy J,
Who rules o'er the land o'Shameen!

The Mail

Oh, the Mail, Oh, the pesky plagued Mail,
How we waited with breath bated
For the Homeside Christmas Mail!
Did it sail? Oh, the ever waited Mail!
How belated underrated
We must always have our mail!

Then the next, the very very next,
And so weekly, we'll wait meekly
For the Homeland Loved-one's best!
Did it sail?
Oh the ever waited Mail!
How belated underrated
Here we live from mail to mail!

Through the years, Oh, the lonely lonely years,
When we melted and we sweltered
In the Tropics, drying tears!
Did it sail? Oh, the ever waited Mail!
How belated underrated
We are dying for our Mail!

First Her mail, Oh, Her lovely lovely Mail,
How we waited and related
To our friends how She would sail!
Did She sail? To, her ever waiting Male?
How belated underrated
But that time we got our Mail!

Then the Folks, Oh, the Gran'ma Gran'pa both,
How they waited events slated
Till the kiddies grew and wrote!
Did it sail? Oh, the ever waited Mail!

Then to school, Oh, the living pulsing school,
How we parted broken hearted
With the kiddies, that's the rule!
Did it sail? Oh, the ever waited Mail!
How belated underrated
But ten times we read their mail!

Then the Wife, Oh, the partner of our life,
Home with children growing children
Or, the doctor and the knife!
Did it sail? Oh, the ever waited Mail!
How belated underrated
We are longing for our Mail!

Then the Bar, Oh, the jolly flowing Bar,
Where the others ask like brothers
How the absent Fam'lies are!
Did it sail? Oh, the ever waited Mail!
How belated underrated
If the Folks could hear us wail!

Then the ague, Oh, the frenzied fever's plague,
How we raved of burning waters
How the Homefolks have delayed!
Did it sail? Oh, the ever waited Mail
How delighted (Who did write it?)
For at last we got our mail!

God Save Our Trees!

(Flora Euro-Orientalis)

TAIPANIA:

(Species Euro-Orientalis
        mammoth colossus honorarium)

Transplanted from the provinces
Of England, Ireland, Scolnd, Wales
And countries of lesser degree,
By the early settlers in the East.

It thrives only in the Foreign Settlements where it is
Deeply rooted to the soil — well saturated, and
Casts its shadows over surrounding shrubbery.
Non-blooming and non-fruit bearing.

E'er sunning its proud foliage
Excepting when transplanted back to its native soil,
Where it shrivels and dies of neglect
Among the giants of the Home forests.

BANKLARK:

(Species Bankum, asinorum
                        paradisa superba)

A dwarfed sapling only produced
From seeds planted in the Western World
And brought to the East
When young and tender.

With slender trunk
Somewhat lacking in core
But holding its head high
And perpetually budding.

Branches rather brittle
And inclined to break before bending
Except when planted near
Its overshadowing species of Taipania

From which it absorbs
Light and moisture —
Seldom shedding its leaves,
Or anything inherited from its native land.

Roots very frail
And easily killed
In rocky soil
Or, when soiled.

BEACHCOMBA:

(Species Uni-Orientalia
                dermis charitas)

A hardy but useless plant
With black core and thick skin
Usually thriving in dark places
And requiring considerable moisture.

Propagates freely in the Far East
And easily grafted to native *flora*.
Very rough in texture,
Casting shadows everywhere.

Leaves variegated
With great power of absorbing
The Eastern national airs —
Exuding offensive odors of ocotra bullata.

Grows en masse in the jungles of cities,
Worthless when living,
Unmarketable when dead —
Polluting the native vegetation.

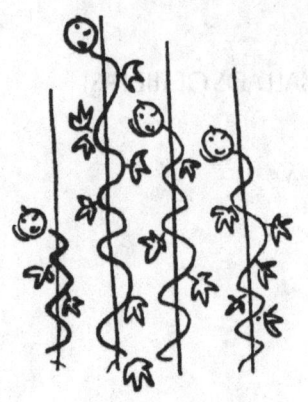

COLONIAL TRAILER:

(Species Civilus subservius
pompousarium)

A creeping and clinging vine
Only rising when supported by
The Empire Oak and other home-grown timber
From which it gets its sustenance:

But in the presence of other vegetation
It stands aloof in the sunshine of
Its own shadow,
Frequently choking with pride.

CONSULERA:

(Species Diplomatis
regal divinarium)

A perennial of oak
Making excellent *sleepers*
For girding the earth and
Extensively used as town posts
for other purposes.

INTRADIA:

(Species Profiteria servitus dispensarium)

One of the more lowly shrubs
But very useful to the formal landscape garden.
Seldom found on club premises but
Used as hedge rows by the near great.

SEADOG:

(Species Saltus saltana
               wandera promiscarium)

A hardy annual, very prolific
Subacidulous sea plant
Occasionally taking root in coast towns
Where its seeds fall freely.

Easily assimilated by the native flora
A very sturdy and life giving plant
Of great interest to scientists
Policemen and bar-maids.

SKYPILOT:

(Species Biblico-creedum sancto sanctorum)

A member of the cactus family
Or century plant.
Everlasting but rarely blooming,
Although always bristling with prickly thorns.

Sometimes used for food by natives
And often carried as a prize by bandits,
Rather poisonous when touched
By irreligious European residents.

Seldom found growing near the proud flora
Of the open ports,
But thriving in the hinterland
Where it propagates freely.

> For other species
> See Catalogue of
> The British Museum
> Or, apply to:
>
> SHAMUS A'RABBITT.

CHINA COAST BALLADS

by

SHAMUS A'RABBITT

Illustrations by "Sapajou"

SHANGHAI
1938

PROLOGUE

This is the book
That shows you where
You'll be if ever
You travel there—

Each place you'll find
On land or sea
Is usually where
It ought to be—

But don't forget—
Suspect a map—
For travel on paper
There's many a trap—

The maps don't show
The gloomy weather
Where fly 'n mosquito
Will get together

To bite and buzz
Around your ears
Until they bring
You home in tears—

*   *   *

Cheer up old friend
When you return
Where you have been
Will memory burn

With tropical sun
And tropical rain—
You'll sing of your fun
In glad refrain.

75

In the East

In the East, in the East
The ever glowing East—
Though greatly overheated
For sport you cannot beat it
Where man can have a jolly time
And "play the game" at least!

In the East 'tis the style—
With credit by the mile
A man can have a debit
Before he knows he has it
And lovely lovely ladies
Will greet him with a smile!

In the East men will fall
Obey the luring call—
Or only get promotion
By death or blind devotion
To Taipans and their pals—
The greatest man of all!

For the East praises ring—
The rovers ever sing—
'Tis baffling, naughty, risky,
Where men enjoy their whiskey
And angel girls will smoke
But never singe their wings!

76

In the East — tropic isles —
The natives clothe in smiles —
With fruit disease foretelling
The flowers bear no smelling
In sizzling heat that mocks
The devil with his wiles!

In the East when it rains
Lurk fevers in the drains —
'Tis sad for those who're going
But happy are they knowing
That memory of friends
And sportsmanship remains!

SHAMUS A'RABBITT

The Goddess Quench

From Shanghai bound for Hongkong
Through sweltering heat we sail —
We dream of Pilsener tankards
On good old Loyal Mail.

We chug down China's coastline
Where salamanders play —
With dripping perspiration
The order of the day.

We hear the clanking fire-irons
As lascars stoke the coal
In Hades' firey furnaces
'Adown the dirty hold.

We hear the rumbling engines
That thump with every stroke —
The parched epiglottis
Now makes us think we'll choke.

Then Fritz the greasy steward
Brings pilsener hot as hell
We order him with orders
To ice and cool it well.

We go with others smiling
Into the hot saloon
For Sunday morning services —
To last from ten till noon.

'Tis thus we go to services
The hottest day at sea
To please the maiden passengers
Whose heroes we would be.

But as the doughty chaplain
Is leading us in prayer
Fritz calls us through the port-hole
And "Cool Beer!" rends the air.

SHAMUS A'RABBITT

The Mystic City

Here all the stars of heaven
Are nestled on the waters
Beneath the sparkling canopy of night —
A thousand brilliant avenues
Come flickering as a welcome —
It is the mystic city that we sight.

As mistress of old Neptune,
She sits upon the ocean —
The goddess of the world her sages plan —
Her head within the heavens
Her feet to stem the tide —
She watches o'er the destiny of man.

Her bosom it has nurtured
From birth to hardy childhood
An Eastern and a Western race's song —
She's wed their art and science
Cementing an alliance —
A glory to the ages — stands Hongkong.

Innocents in the East

O, William was so young and strong
And not inclined to roam
He filled his small-town church with song—
A model boy at home!

Till Destiny on one fine day—
Broke in upon his life
With bids—from China far away—
Farewell to home and wife!

In time he landed at Hongkong—
We bailed him off the ship
And introduced him to our hong
And mysteries of the tip.

Of wine and games and what is worse
He promptly knew a lot
And soon depleted was his purse—
The pace was fairly hot.

One thing that made on him a hit
And filled his life with joy—
The ease with which he signed a chit
The fun it brought—Oh boy!

*   *   *

He couldn't resist
　　The girls of this isle,
Their dark liquid eyes
　　And voluptuous smiles —
From Venus to Mercury
　　He went like a flash
Skyrocketting — plummetting
　　Earthward to crash.

　　　*　　　*　　　*

Then home he went with route selected
　　By us — to save our faces —
And now he's where he's well protected
　　From "dark and evil places" —

Way back within the old home town
　　He lectures every night
And makes the local deacons frown
　　O'er China's need for light!

Dancing Princesses of Hongkong

On a gem of the ocean
Pacific's blue breast
A fairy's fair island
Green coronal crest —

Oft kissing the heavens —
Head moistened with dew
From tear-drops of even'
'Neath skies deepest blue —

Where sunsets like rainbows
O'er waves strewn with pearls —
Reflected in shadows
Two glamourous girls —

Two jewels of motion
Two pearls of the ride
Tokyo nymphs of the ocean
Where mermaidens bide —

These Princesses Charming
The pride of their shore
Had swains ever courting them
E'en by the score—

But they hoped that their fortune
Would earn for their hands
Two valiant courtiers
From "Never-wed" lands.

*   *   *

In mournfulest sadness
I finish my tale—
These girls in their madness
Eschewed every male—

They danced o'er the mountains
Through valleys and glades—
Debarred from love's fountains—
Two lovely old-maids.

SHAMUS A'RABBITT

A Far Eastern Variety

Every little town
Has a ladder of its own.

When Madame de Jay besieged Hongkong
With dash she made a hit —
She vamped the men in many a hong
As victims of her wit.

She ordered gowns made by the score
Of styles defying speech —
For swimming, Madame's bathing suits
Caused riots on the beach!

Of books she read quite all reviews
And prattled off her ware —
She had no time for current news
But made each woman stare.

Poor old de Jay the simple soul
Was entered in the race
To make for every social goal
And follow wifey's pace.

And so he dined and wined and spent
His funds upon all those
Who never spent a single cent
That anybody knows —

They got their first big home — a freak —
Sublet from Hongkongese
But oh, it brought them near the Peak
And made them feel at ease!

'Twas planned about how nice 'twould be
When Madame and her spouse
Would go and shine for all to see
To balls at Government House.

But when the Governor's list came out
Their names did not appear —
The shroffs engaged them in a bout —
To pay would take a year.

And now they're gone — ambitious pair —
Their guests forget their faces —
But soon more climbers will prepare
To come and take their places.

Onward social climbers
Keep on spending more —
Owing butcher baker
And the compradore.

To Sign or Not to Sign

On the far off blue Pacific
There's a tropic isle of dreams —
Where a thirst can be terrific
In the zone of silvery streams.

When discovered in the fifties
With mosquito and the ague
It was thought that aqua vitae
Was the only cure for plague.

So the settlers took to drinking
Liquor famous for the smiles
It produced on spirits sinking
On this gem of Eastern isles

Where they never heard of Volstead
Nor a limit of three miles —
With their courage ever bolstered
By their chits accrued in piles.

'Twas a land of milk and honey
But the milk made dividends
And inn-keepers took no money
For the drinks — which all depends

On a misadvised governor
With an idea in his head —

'Twould be better to abolish
All the chits and pay instead.

The inn-keepers called their lawyers
And the wisest men in town
To protect their lounge and foyers
And keep filthy lucre down.

"We are here to serve good liquor
But we must not ask for pay
And we never like to bicker
With our clients when they say:

'All same boy! You muchee savvy
Makee plenty ice for two—
Chop chop catchee more one bottle
Master makee look see you!' "

Then the Legislative Council
To their chambers they repaired
And it's wise and controversial
The opinions that were aired:

"That our inns are now declining
Is a point we're here to tell—
They must serve their guests on signing
Or this island will be hell!

They must have no peppery clients
And the servants take no cash
Or the public in defiance
Will reduce 'hotels' to smash!"

One old bird contended
That, "Our laws will never serve
To save junor clerks intended
For the dogs—who have the nerve

To sign chits at other places—
I won't mention nor infer—
But our Youth must save their faces
E'en if Life they learn from Her!"

Then His Excellency thinking
To correct these able men
In their logic and their drinking
Made discourse beyond their ken

And instructed all his minions
How to vote on laws like this
Where the ballots and opinions
May be cast to hit or miss.

Lo – the sun went down and darkened
And the moon shed not its light
With the islanders disheartened
O'er the world's most hopeless plight!

SHAMUS A'RABBITT

The Absent-minded Sport

O, the joy of being careless —
And oft absent-minded too —
As a boy they made me fearless
Of the things I had to do!

When my time came to be married —
In an absent-minded way —
Through the days and weeks I tarried
And forgot the wedding day —

Then my girl engaged detectives
And they saw me to the church
As she thought my mind defective
I might leave her in the lurch.

But before the thing was over
And the choir began to sing —
Then somehow did I discover
I'd forgot the wedding ring.

All the answers I recited
And 'twas so the knot was tied
For you see I was excited
Or you bet I would have lied!

O, I never can get even
With my wife and her refrain—
Her advice I'm e'er receiv'n—
It has driven me insane!

"You must not forget your money—
And be careful on the street—
Don't forget to kiss me honey—
Or, mislay your pearly teeth!"

O, these words are ever ringing
In my tired and weary ears
While the Missie goes on singing
"Dear, forget me not," in tears!

Then I came out to the tropics
Where I thought I needn't mind
E'en forgetting current topics
In the hot and fearsome grind!

And I rented an apartment
In the Past-her-house Hotel
But forgot to pay the house-rent
And the landlord gave me hell!

So you see I got in trouble
As I couldn't say a word—
I forgot my teeth and "bubble"—
Was all the landlord heard!

Now my wife is on the war-path
As she says I'm indiscreet—
For I had a funny accident
While looking for my teeth.

> I forgot my name and number
> As I wandered far and wide
> And disturbed the peace and slumber
> Of a neighbor and his bride.

'Tis the worst of matrimony
But if wifey goes to court—
I'll forget the alimony
As an absent-minded sport!

As the Better Half Thinketh

The other day
I had a long talk
With a wonderful girl.

She told me in a casual way
What she expects of her friend husband —
And this is only part of what she said:

"Ne'er a short-story man
Who finishes life at the altar —
Instead — a stirring serial;

No summer flower
To bloom upon the honeymoon,
But a perennial of oak;

A gentleman at core
But this alone is not enough,
The outward signs as well he must possess;

You know we have ideals,
But, close at hand, our senses reign supreme —
Yes, even with our disillusionment;

Though dress is not the only thing,
I note when they're in love they're groomed so
    very well —
'Twas so with mine when he was courting me;

    If drinking makes him more refined,
      Why then 'tis right to drink —
    But, otherwise go off the stuff for life;

    For manly sports he should go in —
      To take him out of doors —
        Be not a slave of shop.

      Oh, yes, I like shop talk
    If 'tis the same his steno listens to —
      Of profits, not all losses;

To pay my bills with airs that he puts on
When meeting debts of honor
Or monthly chits at club;

To be a good provider,
Or a good husband — that I know
Is but a duty. Don't you see?

He should be something more —
Well, say a lover and a friend —
A gallant first of all to me!

Then other girls
In admiration would he green —
'Tis this that adds a zest to life.

Respectful to his wife of course,
But this alone would make him very dull —
He should then be my hero too.

To treat my friends as his
And his to let me treat as mine
And that's the kind of man to love for life.

The others, well,
They make a good wife wicked and —
A bad one but respectable!"

Boy!
All same,
Large glass!

The Slacker

O, Cupid, where art thou
When little Joe next door
Doth ask his playmate if she'll be
His wife forevermore?

O, Cupid, where art thou
When Mamma says, "'Tis best for you
My little sweetheart angel girl,
To marry him (he is so well-to-do)?"

O, Cupid, where art thou
When Jim (or John) receives promotion,
And booked to far Hongkong
Doth sing of love's devotion?

O, Cupid, where art thou
When preachers quote to see
If any man can shew just cause —
Why didst thou not save me?

Didst thou not know
About the seed of love implanted in the breast
Of someone else? Who made it so —
Was it at thy behest?

Didst thou not know
When I within my teens was wed
That in my best friend's wedded mate
Was growing then this seed to make me
    wish me dead?

Didst thou not know —
Somewhere, sometime, when I was off
    my guard,
This seed would blossom forth
To make life hard?

Dost thou not know
O'er half the world doth blame thee
For wedding bells that ring too soon?
Blue-bells of love that ne'er can be!

O, Cupid, where art thou
And all thy myriad angels out of tune
Who come and sing their songs of love
At night — too late, and not at lovely noon

O, Cupid, where art thou
Whene'er some lowly sub upon thy staff
Pours out the poppy's wormwood on our lives
Disguised as honey, making e'en
    the Devil laugh?

Thou slacker, Cupid, wake and set to right
All thy mistakes — the souls forlorn
Who meet through thy neglect too late
And wish they'd ne'er been born!

Shore Leave

Said Captain Sam, U.S.S. "Mary Ann"
To Commander William Holmes:
"A summer day in Hongkong Bay
Was made for lazy bones."

Commander Holmes of the British Squad —
A damn fine chap was he —
The ship he had was the prize each lad
Would fight for on the sea.

Said Sam, "My men are restless when
They're cooped up over here."
'Twas Holmes reply, "My men near die
From heat here every year."

"We go to sea with Dry Rule naught three"
Said the Yankee with a wink —
"Though against the rules made only
    for fools
What say you to a drink?"

"All right 'old top' I don't mind a drop"
Said Holmes, "I think 'tis right
This spell we'd break if our men should take
Their joint shore leave tonight."

"Agreed," said Sam with a hel-uv-a slam
Then smiles rolled o'er their cheeks —
And all that night with a hel-uv-a fright
Hongkong turned out the Sikhs.

(The Hongkong Force gives a natural course
Of lessons when whey teach
Each drunken Gob — though they have some job —
When Yanks and Limeys beach.)

For days and days in the tropical rays
The sun beat in the court —
While Captain Sam as meek as a lamb
And Holmes the same old sort

103

Would bail their men with gravity when
The Court of the British Isles
Had fined both ships for broken lips—
Though black eyes brought them smiles.

Now summer's gone and they've moved
    along—
Both ships are far away—
Up where I'll tell 'tis cold as hell—
In Vladivostok Bay.

Their fighting men will scrap now 'n then
To find the better one —
But orders with them are orders e'en when
The hard day's work is done.

The shake's the thing when they leave the ring —
A rule that means fairplay —
They fight and sing with a hel-uv-a fling
In the Anglo-Saxon way.

The Night Boat from Hongkong to Canton

We leave Hongkong resplendent
With planets in gay attire
Each glittering flashing brilliant
A guiding beacon fire—

Inverted bowl of the heavens
Clove by the Milky Way—
Star-life in teeming millions
Illume the stellar day.

With Hongkong Isle behind us—
A cluster of baby stars
Reflects upon the waters
The paths that will be ours.

Here gathered from all nations
We meet the East and West—
A group of all professions
Gold not our only quest.

We feel the boat's pulsations—
Propellers against the tide—
As steaming up the channel
Past phantom junks we glide.

Past lights of old Cap See Mun
With channel lights beneath—
Gray mountains in the distance
Float on a vapory sheet.

We pass the grim Two Brothers—
Two islands all alone—
Like sentinels ever watching
This danger-ridden zone.

The Sikh guards armed with carbines—
Be-turbanned—grim—upright—
Pace to-and-fro while watching
For pirates through the night.

Between barred decks sleep natives
Packed humans—like sardines—
With hawkers selling medicines
For all their ailing dreams—

A living struggling cargo
Bent on its joy—its crime—
A protoplasmic wonder—
A floating speck of time.

The night wears on in cadence
With thumping of the steam—
We come to the Canton Delta
Cut through the yellow stream—

Soft molten rolling cloud racks
Fill spaces overhead
Reflect the dancing light beams
From gold to darkest red—

Clouds bank the walled horizon
With weird and grotesque forms—
On rolling hills are ruined
Pagodas of the storms—

Comes purple dawn with battlements
Upholding Eastern sky—
Late dewy shreds e'er melting
As silvery clouds pass by.

Cocks crow—the dogs give warning—
The cocks they crow again—
Floats lazy smoke with morning
To greet the dawn's refrain.

We enter Canton's river
But ere we've time to stop
Lithe water folk swarm over
Our decks, our stern, our top—

Mad jabbering like monkeys—
Man, woman, maid and child—
Dense teeming hoards of Canton
Resound like jungles wild.

Here time began for age of man—
Here time will cease to be—
Here life goes on without a plan
A separate entity—

Here all things are exotic and
We feel exotic too—
Here mystery's round the corner and
There's zest to what we do—

Here dreamers may forget the world
And foreigners be kings—
Here's where the commonplace is strange
With topsy turvy things.

SHAMUS A'RABBITT

At Anchor

On Canton's delta estuary
Storm-tossed junks at anchor ride—
Sea pilgrims droning sanctuary
Music of the lapping tide—

Their swarthy mariners in song—
At rest from battles long and hard—
Through typhoons—with their hearts as strong
As seasoned shrouds fast to the yard—

Sea hawks whose wakes around the world
Have glistened in the sun now on their rails—
Their golden woven sheets enfurled
And laid to rest their battered sails.

Suspended are the yards on every mast
That once was rooted in the forest gloom
But now to keel and decks and rigging fast—
Bestript—no longer called upon to bloom—

Masts kist by rain adown their naked sides—
Caressed by winds that sing the songs they know—
Borne on the inward and the outward tides
On phantoms of the dee—they come and go—

To loom at evening o'er the river's sheet—
At rest between their voyages remain—
Till newer cargo stored within the fleet—
Their silence changed to flapping wings again.

These ghostly ships have eyes that never sleep—
As partly fish and partly bird in form—
Ne'er rising from the bosom of the deep—
Embraced by sea—birds winged upon the storm.

What stories could these sturdy vessels tell—
What calms and storms and wildest piracies?
Beyond our dream-adventure's wierdest hell—
These sailing junks that go down to the seas!

The Sanctimonious Griffin

Sad is the view
When angels hath
Revealed anew
The stony path!

O Billy was a gentle boy
An unassuming lad
Who smoked sweet-scented cigarettes
With jas'min tea when bad!

To picnics he was always asked
And ushered at the church
Whilst we and other huskies were
Left outside in the lurch.

Till finally so good was he —
So evangelical —
He tried to save men of the sea
And sampan girls from hell.

He preached against all human joys
And nightly could be seen
When reading Scripture to the boys
And girlies off Shameen.

But soon we saw the prayer meetings
Called by Billie Boy
Attended less and less until
They left the sleek Ho Toy —

A daughter of the outcast hordes
Defeated long ago
And driven to a water life
Where Canton rivers flow —

She kowtowed to her gods each day
The Chin Chin gods we see
When browsing through the muck and mire
Of temples near Sha-kee —

A number-one wee Chin Chin girl —
No Christian joss was she —
But Ho — she had a business eye.
And so she caught Bill-ee!

  The sons of Han
  And daughters too
  May worship as
  The Christians do —
  Their hearts remain
  In Buddha's care —
  More vital is
  Their daily fare.

Neptune's Daughter

The signals are flying
Red balls on the mast—
The wind is now sighing—
The sails scurry past—

But all on the "Margot"
Are ready to leave
The harbor of Canton
For Hongkong at eve—

We pull up the anchor
Each man of our crew
Stands by for the battle
As sailormen do—

Then scudding the reaches
We head for Whampo—
Through shrouds the wind screeches—
To eastward we go—

But ere we reach Bocco—
The forts at the bite—
The typhoon is howling
And black is the night—

115

The skipper is singing
Enjoying the storm —
Above roaring billows
We hear his wild song:

"O, batter my windows blow and blow
Ye winds from over the seas
Tonight I'm snug where'er ye go
Ensconced below with ease —

Whenever ye shake and rattle the pane
And tear at my cabin door
And bring to your aid my old friend rain
I know that we've met before —

Last year when ye tore my sails away
And left me to wallow the sea
Ye gave me the thrill I feel today
To stir up the soul in me!

But where O, vagrant have ye been
Through all the seasons round
What sails have ye shattered and torn
since then
What ships have ye cast a-ground?

And why do I love your fiery teeth
That hiss and spit in the gale
O, is it because my soul ye greet
With something that will not quail?

Something that's left of primitive man
That's handed down to me
Something of battle which never can
From brute in man be free?

Why rise and fall and lash and flay
And shake and writhe and roll
O, why more ugly by night than day
And why do ye take such toll?

Perchance ye are kin to man and beast
From North and South and West
And others who sing when from the East
Your songs come deep in the breast —

Songs that we sing whene'er ye blow
Songs that are wild and free
Songs of a life lived long ago
Songs for a man o' the sea!"

*   *   *

The skipper's daughter
A child of the sea
Though only twelve summers
A brave lass is she —

E'en tossed by the billows
And wracked by the storm
A dream-child so fearless
She thinks of no harm.

117

Tonight she is restless
With mind to the waves
A child of the elements
Like winds as they rave —

She stops her father's singing
With wild piercing cry:
"Oh, Dad, someone's calling
Someone's going to die!"

"Still child," cries the Skipper,
"Thou wilt ever dream!"
But hardly he's spoken
When we hear a scream.

With searchlight on waters
All eyes o'er the sides
Where Neptune's gay daughters
Unlashed a thousand tides —

"'Tis there!" cries the Skipper
"Don't jam the life boats!
Here — here — I see it —
'Tis someone — it floats!

Now steady men steady —
A damn nasty night!
O, pull ye beggars
Just there to the right!

Hard on the oars men —
A slip and we're damned!
Hold there hold the devil —
Another inch and we're rammed!

I've got it! 'Tis coming!
Hard on that part oar!
My God — 'tis a woman! —
There now — once more!"

In the Skipper's strong arms
Is a limp — wretched form
With face turned to heaven
That seems to lull the storm.

*   *   *

Below first aid is given
With warmth and cheer we bring her
The best from our rough stores
Served by our captain's daughter.

For hours twixt life and death
She hovers in delirium —
The sad sad tale from her
Strikes on our hearts a requiem!

"A lady of honor and wealth was I
With home and husband too —
But while upon the Fatshan's deck
My hushand's arms around my neck

I told him that I'd like to die
Into the sea I'd like to glide
To leave forever my husband's side
Commit a glorious suicide —

And the damn man threw me overboard!"

Shadows

A shadow gay I crave to be—
A merry shadow on the sea—
To scamper after ships at night—
To blot the winking stars from sight—
To roll the clouds around the moon—
With other shadows hide at noon—

With shadows lurk in derelicts
As silent as the stygian Styx—
With shadows haunt the slimy decks
Of sunken craft and cast up wrecks—
With shadows of all who went to sea—
All shadows of what I dreamt to be.

Dreaming on the Way to Old Nanning

On the way to old Nanning
Young engineers we dreamed
That we'd change the map and everything
(While ploughing up the stream)
   O the blessings we would bring
   To the folk of old Nanning!

As we tugged from drab Wuchow —
Si Kiang up sixty feet
There we planned our bridges — how —
They'd cross where Fo Ho meet —
   Build cities for a king
   On the way to old Nanning!

From Bat-Ma the river wide
Will flood the valleys low
But the waters we would tide —
A million horse-power show —
   We'd make the anvils ring
   On the way to old Nanning!

We'd construct at dire Sum Chow
Upon her wooded hills
Broad green terraces — allow
Health balms to bear no ills —
    Fair courts and schools we'd bring
    On the way to old Nanning!

On the plains around Kwai Yuen
Abound pastoral lands
Here in justice men would soon
Convert the roving bands —
    Put bandits on the wing
    On the way to old Nanning!

On the way to old Nanning
Tibet and far Yunnan
Would then market everything
O'er routes for maid and man
    To travel on and sing
    On the way to old Nanning!

         *   *   *

On the way from old Nanning
We left our concrete mixers
There to rust with tools and fixtures
To mark the graves of comrades
    Whose voices no more ring
    On the way from old Nanning.

On the way from old Nanning
Where once lived forty millions
There the bandits — vultures hover
O'er the plains and o'er the river
    Death and desolation cling
    On the way from old Nanning.

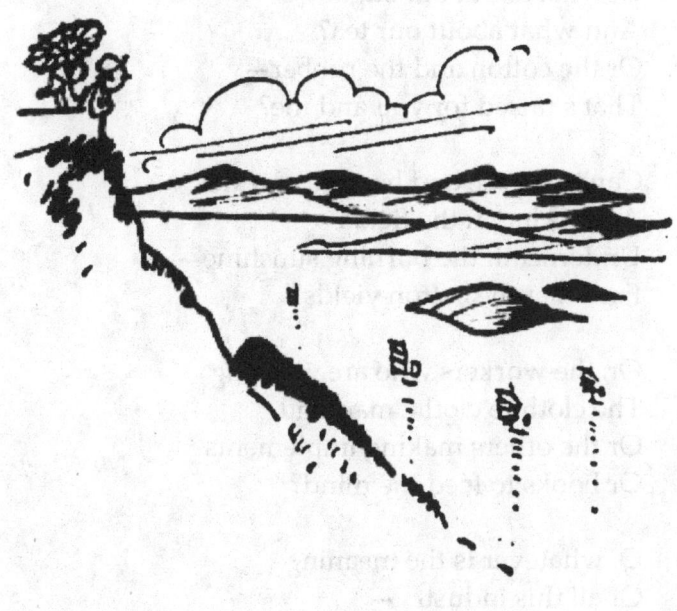

"Go Ye Forth and Spread the Gospel"

O, what about our sugar
And what about our tea?
Or the cotton and the rubber—
That's raised for you and me?

Can't you see and hear the darkies
A-working in the fields—
Underneath the burning sunshine—
For what the cotton yields?

Or, the workers who are weaving
The cloth to clothe mankind
Or the others making implements
Or books to feed the mind?

O, whatever is the meaning
Of all this industry—
That will struggle for a living—
Each day for you and me?

'Tis the industry at home and
The industry abroad—
Whether serving God or Mammon—
That is all in one accord—

The evangelist's hand-maiden—
The merchant's ready prop—
Without this firm foundation
Our world would surely stop!

"Go ye forth and spread the Gospel!"
Are words that we know well
But how would this teaching prosper—
If we'd nothing we could sell?

The Other Fellow

We've often heard
That fools' faces
Are always seen
In public places
But have we heard
Of all the cases
Of fools we'd send
To other places?

There's the fool says we resemble
A man in Timbuctoo —
And informs our friends assembled
Of tricks that man could do —

And the fool who makes excuses
Not asking us to dine
When we still recall abuses
Once caused by his "old" wine —

And the man who holds up dinner
Is king of fools' estate —
What we'd do to such a sinner
We cannot here relate —

One who's late to concert coming
And has an inside seat —
Or, who's dined so well — starts humming —
That kind is hard to beat

Oh, alas, 'tis such a pity
That fools cause so much fuss
And we wonder why our city
Can't have more folk like us!

    Of asses there
    Are many kinds
    But biggest on the street
    Are those who underrate
    The minds
    Of other men they meet.

SHAMUS A'RABBITT

How Do You Read Your Paper?

O, how do you read your paper —
In the morning or at night?
Do you read it like your neighbor
Who will ne'er do things a-right?

Do you glance o'er all the headlines
And then pounce upon your prey
To disclose the latest scandal
Or the horrors of the day?

Do you first look for the cables
In from Germany and France —
Or within the social column,
For the latest silly dance?

Do you swallow editorials
And the governmental bills?
Do you read the testimonials
For the kidney cures and pills?

Are you ever caught by titles
Like — "What Every Woman Knows" —
But to find at end instructions
For removing corns from toes?

Do you read the "wanted" columns—
For absorbing human woes—
Learning how the suffering millions
Have to live—how, no one knows?

Or, the latest London market price
Of rice or bonds and stocks?
Or, the movements of the steamers
That will put up at our docks?

When I look at those around me—
I am sure that I can tell—
By the marking on their features—
Of the page that each reads well.

I can tell the crusty fellow
Who will read with frenzied ire
But finds "nothing in the paper"
And then throws it in the fire.

And of one thing I am certain—
Such a welcome sight to greet—
'Tis the happiness of children
Which demands the funny sheet.

O, the paper is a "creature"
With a great and wondrous sight—
It is born anew each morning
And it dies again at night!

Yes, it caters to the masses
And the masses for it pay —
It must satisfy all classes
In their each and every way.

Very often do I wonder
What another man can find
Looking in the "useless" columns
That will never suit my mind.

Then there's one thing I remember —
That this world's a funny place —
And I know what's sauce for others
Will not suit my acid face.

The Call Primeval

O would I were a flying squirrel
Or e'en a chimpanzee—
To swing from branches overhead
And glide from tree to tree—
To hang on boughs with ne'er a care
But plucking fruit for mate—
To chase and catch—embrace, ensnare—
In this primeval state—
Or better far—a panther lithe
To spring upon my prey
To roam alone the hills at night—
To browse away the day—
Or e'en a tiny warbling bird
To fly about and sing
Such music as the world's ne'er heard—
To charm each living thing!
These thoughts don't come whene'er I stroke
My beard—or roam afar—
They're thoughts that come whene'er I smoke
My pipe or my cigar.

Predigestination

Please pardon my suggestion
I've mental indigestion
Persuing all the "digests" of the day —
The digest — literary —
The readers' commentary —
And digests of what politicians say.

'Tis woe unto the reader
Who must now be a speeder
Through mazes of our governmental bills —
In tabloid form they hit us
With predigested jitters —
Hell's blazes of our current history's ills.

I suggest in compensation
We digest our conversation
To a minimum of what will do us harm —
While talking to my neighbor —
He used not sword nor sabre
But talked away my trusty starboard arm.

The Archeologist of the Breakfast Table

I've always envied excavators
Who travel far and wide
To hunt the dinosaur's eggs
In deserts where they hide —

To open tombs of Egypt's kings
To pry upon their mummies
To rob their queens of wedding rings
To dig and dig for dummies —

To visit Bali and Sumatra
And steal the natives' wives —
Or scale the needle Cleopatra —
Such men lead noble lives.

I've envied Peary, Byrd and Nansen
For going to the Poles
To see the sun for months on end —
Inspiring are such souls.

I've envied those who sail the seas
And visit southern isles —
To loaf and dream in summer breeze —
To bask in sunny smiles.

I too have travelled far alone
I've searched through cranny and nook
To find the rarest species known —
One who returns a book!

Adventure

Adventure's fine—
I will admit
That I am very
Fond of it—

Detective tales
Make me respond
To one who takes
A million bond—

The stories new or tales of old
On land or on the sea
Of buccaneers and pirates bold
Have great appeal for me—

*   *   *

E'en my Aunt Mary
Prudish spinster
Still hides behind her fan
Avoiding all that
She thinks sinister
Such as every passing man—And yet the old girl
Is a brick
She scolds me when
I'm taking
One night off
But gets a "kick"
From tales of wild
Law breaking.

135

SHAMUS A'RABBITT

Wanted: A Name!

In our comity of nations
There's a very ancient race
Ever famous for pendragons
Whose fair deeds they would efface—

By a name that they might fit on
To old Albion or Brit
Which would never sound like Brit-on
And a Britisher's not it.

Would Britonian or Britishite
Pronounce with greater ease—
Britishonian might be all right
But never Britishese!

Then there is the Albionite—
And this name alone might please—
Or, again we may call and write
Them down as Albionese!

But the Scottish and the Irish
And the Welsh who'd take to Celt,
Would they not object to English
And make their objections felt?

Whether Anglican or Welshman
Or, Erinite or Scot—
It is certain that the Irish
Won't give up the name they've got!

Spare the Trees

O, Woodman, spare the tree,
That here doth spread its gentle shade —
Whose gnarled trunk so gloriously
Bespeaks the hearts of man and maid!

When long ago for good or bad,
In bark so young and tender —
They carved their names, the maid and lad —
He swore he would defend her

Against the wiles and ways of man,
Throughout their lives to be —
So true the compact ran —
And witnessed by this tree.

O, Woodman, spare the tree,
With such a hallowed tale —
Beneath these branches silently
Have I grown old and pale!

Alas, the boy who carved for me,
(Against the wiles of men —)
Initials in this lovely tree —
He left me there and then

Although he pledged that we should live
Together for alway —
Was it the kiss I did not give
That sent him far away?

        *   *   *

O, Woodman, fell the tree
With others that portend
Our hopeless dreams quite shamelessly
With carvings that pretend

To bind a troth twixt man and maid,
And place them side by side
To keep their shadows and their shade
From e'er a would-be bride!

And when collected — all of those
Encarved for troths — a token —
As many will you have — who knows —
As there are hearts — not — broken!

Dignity

O waddle on, O waddle on
Through season's rain or shine
Ye penguins have a waddle that
I wish to God were mine—

O waddle on, O waddle on
Through weather foul or fair
Ye penguins' waddle waddle keeps
Your heads up in the air—

O waddle on, O waddle on
Ye feathered dignitaries
If ye but had eye glasses on
Ye'd look like secretaries—

O waddle on, O waddle on
Like congressmen on ice
Or penguinistic senators
Ye look so very nice—

O waddle on, O waddle on
I wish I knew your thoughts
Ye wear the robe of dignity
Perhaps you're full of naughts —

O waddle on, O waddle on
Ye stand the winter's gaff
And look both wise and stupid but
Your waddle makes me laugh.

Nero the Hero

Through centuries
Since Rome was burned
The books record
What Nero earned—

Old Nero's blamed
Because of harm
That came to Rome
Sans fire alarm—

'Twas started by
His adversaria
Because he played
His Stradivaria—

But merely sincerely
He made a mistake
And earned he quite dearly
His rep as a rake—

Instead of his fiddle
If bowed with his beads
He'd called on the firemen
To witness his deeds

Commanded the Romans
To kneel and to pray
From ashes would Nero
Be hero today.

Tropical Ecstasy

When flickering sunbeams
Dance o'er the grass
Make tinkling ice
Within the glass
A symphony
No tongue can tell —
That's parched like
A burning hell —
We see the grass
Turn green to brown
And gulp our cooling
Liquor down —
We sing of the sea
We sing of the sky
We sing of the planets
That pass us by —
We speak of the wonders
Of nature and man —
The vastness of China —
The charm of Japan —
But greater, O greater
Than any of these
Is the burning sun setting
Behind the trees.

Absence

My friend hath gone across the sea,
And homeward I return,
The sea gull's cry depresses me
The foaming billows churn —
   'Tis Fortune's sorry turn
   To take away my friend.

The ocean wide, the drifting tide
Are placed between us now,
And silently as time will glide
To Fate's decree I bow —
   To pain I must allow
   From absence of my friend.

Each echo is awakening
The deepest thoughts I know,
For every space left void doth ring
With music soft and low —
   All tones that come and go
   Now shape thee — absent friend.

Of thy great presence I'm bereft
And now I see and feel
That everything thou touched and left
Thy imprint doth reveal —
   E'en though I try — conceal
   This vision of thee, friend.

The open door, the empty chair
The books thou touched with love
And every whisper in the air
And every star above—
   The paths we used to rove
   All now recall thee—friend.

My prayers forever on will be—
Though years between us burn—
That fortune ever smile on thee
And hasten thy return—
   May Neptune once more churn
   The waves—Retum, O, friend.

Exiles

On tropical bays, Far Eastern Seas
Where mystery isles belong —
The rumbling surf in symphonies
Accompanies our song.
In vibrant tones our hearts e'er sing
Enchanting Homeland lays —
Sweet and low and murmuring
To cheer our lonely days —

With lays of olden melody
And childhood lullabies
Our souls are brought in harmony
With worlds of great emprise.
We drift afar in space where dwell
The tones of every glow
Reflected from the sunset spell
We longing exiles know —

And vibrant to the sonant strings
Attuned to every heart —
Are chords released on friendship's wings
For loved ones far apart —
With songs that are akin to all
In tune with nature's best —
Vibrating voices ever call
Our heart-strings home to rest.

The Family Shrine

When travelling up and down this
   godless land
Through Yangtze valley towns and
   everywhere
There looms the family shrine on every
   hand
Where spirits of the ancestors repair.

This link the Orientals keep, alas!
With those who've passed and those
   who are no more—
We Occidentals leave the thoughts of
   past
And worship what for us life hath in
   store.

The family shrines—by all the types
    we know—
Of sturdy mariner or gentle born—
In sacred memory where'er we go—
Are photographs of those from whom
    we're torn.

Dreamline

The streamline car
The streamline boat
The streamline sink
The streamline coat—

The streamline train
The streamline baby
Then still remains
The streamline lady—

The streamline spouse
For a streamline life
In a streamline house
With a streamline wife—

The streamline face
A streamline skin
Now haunts the space
I travel in—

Old-fashioned are
My base desires
I like the good
Old-fashioned fires—

Old-fashioned fires
That burn within
A rugged face
With sunburned skin—

A girl with lines
No eel would crave
But lines that make
Me misbehave—

Lines that make me
Dream by day
The Dreamlines that
A lover may

Feel a lover's
Loving thrill
And pay a lover's
Loving bill—

Speed mania rules
It is now said
But some things
Are best delayed—

Delayed for dreaming
As of yore
Of love as love
Was loved before—

The streamline girl's
A sight to see
But the dreamline girl's
The girl for me.

SHAMUS A'RABBITT

Our Synthetic World

Today is yesterday's future
And tomorrow's past.

The synthetic age
Is here at last
The dream of sages
And alchemists past—

The dreams of old
Are reality
With synthetic gold
And synthetic tea.

Laboratories
And not the field
Our harvest seeds
In tabloids yield:

Our synthetic wood
And synthetic cloth—
Our synthetic food
And synthetic moth—

The Bomby moth
Is not required
For rayon got
The silk-worm fired —

The lamb no longer
Need be shorn
For staple fibre
Will be worn —

E'en though each
And every stitch
Will carry it's
Synthetic itch.

With synthetic joy —
Synthetic gin —
We'll next employ
Synthetic sin.

SHAMUS A'RABBITT

The Wisdom of Satan

Missie Bubbling Well
In Hop Sing's shop —
"Wanchee one piecee meat
No wanchee bone
No wanchee grizzle
No wanchee fat
No wanchee skin — —"
Hop Sing talkee —
"Missy me thinkee
More better you catchee
One piecee egg."

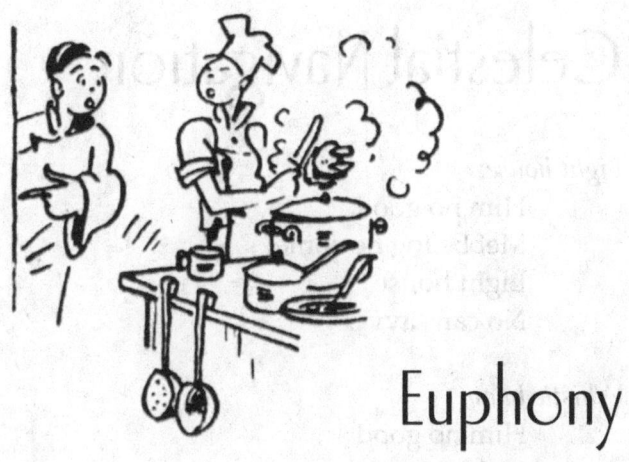

Euphony

Missy to Number One boy
One day talkee
"Today you talkee Cook
Catchee one piecee pigeon
Dress in aspic
Puttee casserole" —
(Boy him bime — bye talkee)
"Missy me talkee Cook
Cook him talkee me
Velly sorry
No can catchee today
One piecee castor oil."

Celestial Navigation

Light house:
>Him no good
>Mebbe fog he come
>Light house
>No can savvy.

Whistle buoy:
>Him no good
>Mebbe typhoon come
>Whistle buoy
>No can hear.

Fog Horn:
>Him no good
>Plenty time
>I makee him blow
>Fog he all same come
>Stay water top side.

Shanghai Waif

"No mamma
No papa
No whisky soda
No chow "

Pierced the air
And pierced the din
Of the Shanghai crowd
On road Nankin!

"No mamma
No papa
No brother
No sister "

While nimble fingers
And nimble hand
Juggled four knives
Near the chow-chow stand.

"No mamma
No papa
No dolla
No chow"

Came through the crowd
To the passers by
From the Chinese girl
With a naughty eye.

   "No mamma
    No papa
    No whisky soda
    No chow."

Jostled by rickshaws
She cursed them aloud
And juggled four knives
Amusing the crowd.

   "No mamma
    No papa
    No brother
    No sister"

Then a big Sikh
Policeman's
Baton
Just missed her.

"No mamma
No papa
No dolla
No chow"

The knives went like magic
Despite the mock bow —
Juggling four chop sticks
She wrinkled her brow —

"No mamma
No papa
No whiskey soda
No chow"

She slipped across
A sailor's path —
A sailor drunk
Who swore his wrath —

"No mamma
No papa
No whiskey soda
No chow"

"Get out of my way
Or I'll kick your pants."
With grimace she said—
"No have got pants."

   "No mamma
   No papa
   No whiskey soda
   No chow "

Ten cents please!

Good Old World!

I hear
The world's all wrong
And I must confess
That I am in
A hell of a mess

For I have helped
To make the thing
Just to hear
My children sing—
I worked for years
And I was busy
But now the damn thing
Makes me dizzy—

With the grain
God made the chaff
And now nor God
Nor man can laugh
At old or new
Mythology
Without fouling
Ideology —

We've prison bars
And stripes for humor
Supprest beneath
The festering tumor
Of unbalanced budgets —
Of unpaid bills —
Destructire gadgets —
Expensive ills.

The world's not wrong —
I must confess —
'Tis man who's in
A hell of a mess.

The Thoroughbred

The head erect
A charm about the neck
Of lines that make a poem—
Sensitive the nostrils
And well defined the nose
The head is something all its own
In every graceful pose;

The eyes that gaze at me
With such a knowing look
Attract me with their gentleness—
The clearness of a brook—
Sometimes these eyes
Are springs of liquid
Deep as is the soul—
At least
They look that way to me!

The delicate and web-like tracery
Of veins beneath the skin
E'er pulsate with the rise and fall
Of heart throbs from within—
Why say more
Of one whose very presence
Is a charm
Inspiring
E'en the roughest men
To shield such grace from harm?

The artists of all times
Have died to win for art
The secret of these lines of limbs
That draw us to the heart
Of these rare queens of sport—
E'er making sport for kings—
And yet—a stable boy
To kingship may arise
In thought
And in his actions by
The light within
A thoroughbred's
Or lovely woman's eyes.

Beauty and the Beast

She whom I love I must not love;
That she loves me I know—
With love as pure as purest gold
Or as the driven snow.

A tough old dog of war am I,
That she loves me's a shame—
An ugly brute near twice her age
And still she'd take my name.

The more I tell her 'tis not right,
Protest my wickedness—
The more she swears that as my wife
She'd bring me happiness.

O, what to do with maid like this,
Is more than I can tell—
For when she is as old as I—
I'll be as old as hell!

SHAMUS A'RABBITT

Many Happy Returns

Come drink with me but one cup more,
To purge out hearts of sorrow —
We know not what the dawn may store
Within the sad tomorrow!

*   *   *

Dash for a train and make it at last —
Rush through the rain with towns flying past —
Walk on the ceiling — something's gone wrong
Things topsy turvy where I belong!

Out at a station — jump on again —
Cling to the windows — batter my brain —
Jump off a bridge and slide down a precipice
Over a ridge to light on a pretty miss —

Rest on the hand of the maiden so fair
Then try to stand on her sweet scented hair —
Soon brushed aside when the winds come along —
Away on the tide of man's busy throng —

Attracted by odors, dash to a scene
Where rots a carcass of putrid gangrene —
Here try to enter the mouth and the eyes —
Blocked by the buzzing of blue bottle flies —

See smoke arise far over the wood —
Mecca for flies, a home to the good —
Off with a breeze as straight as an arrow —
Over the trees in track of a sparrow —

Dinner is cooking with fragrance of spice
Know without looking, in there it is nice —
Wait at the screen till someone comes out —
Must not be seen or I'll get a clout —

At last in the pantry, my hunger to break —
Delectable sundries for me to partake —
Lo, what is this that I am caught in?
Stepping I miss the skin I was wrought in:

A voice from the distance thundering now,
Angry insistence making a row!
Blink with a blink, half open my eyes —
Think with a think, I see the blue skies —

Gads, what a train of thoughts in my head:
The voice bawls again, "You sleep like
   the dead.
Get up lazy beggar, the house is a sight —
Wish you many happy returns — of the
   night"

*   *   *

When the head is hot
And lips are parched
And thoughts of the night are with you —
It is time you got
A sip and searched
For a chip of the block that hit you!

Alibi Julius E.

O, Julius E, as a model he'd be,
And never tell a lie —
When caught 'red handed' he'd
    say when landed,
"So help me God, I'll die!"

O, Julius E, he would flirt would he
With the girls who'd pass him by —
And never admit it, e'en when he was pitted
With the wink still in his eye.

So Julius E, as he never could be
Found guilty of anything harmful —
Was caught in a whirl and he married the girl —
And say but she was an armfull.

O, Julius E, he would practice, would he
An innocent look on his features —
Whene'er he came in he would look without sin,
The saddest and queerest of creatures.

So Julius E, of innocence he
Was guilty and caught in his lair —
No longer he'd try tell his alibi
And so he gave up in dispair.

Then Julius E, at last we could see
Had made up his mind he would die —
But when he reached Hell, he only could tell
He came with his sin's alibi.

Old Bill

When Bill was young
And full of pep
He tried his best
To make a "rep" —
But ne'er a "rep"
Bill made — you see —
His youth and pep
Went on a spree!
But now Old Bill
Is good — is he —
He never goes
Out on a spree —
And yet he cannot
Make a "rep "
Because he hasn't
Got the pep!

An Appreciation of Nothing

Nothing is something
With a hole around it
And through the hole
There's a ribbon in it
And when you tie the ribbon it's gone —
That's nothing
That's nothing —

Love at a summer resort
Engaged in by some as a sport
To others —
That's nothing
That's nothing —

A girl sends a boy
For naught but sheer joy
For-get-me-nots
Forget-me-nots
That's nothing
Just nothing —

The boy sends a girl roses
And pretends and proposes
That's nothing
That's nothing —
The hell it is!

SHAMUS A'RABBITT

Thank God for That

Poets, turks and bachelors
Have in their verses sung —
That virtues of the many
Are not contained in one —
But ne'er was the poet
Turk, bachelor withal —
Thanking lucky stars like I
My girl has not the faults of all.

Why Not?

Why should her eyes not be red,
Or salmon, apricot or pink
E'en lilac, heliotrope, or purple shades
Would add a little zest to life—I think.

Brutus Was an Honorable Man!

I read each "wanted column" ad
And what I find there makes me sad—
With head-lines listing "Lost and Found"
(So honest does this caption sound—)
I read and find it is a frost—
All of the "ads" are items lost!

This Revolving World

Has fortune passed you by this year —
If so good friend pray have no fear —

For like the years that pass us by
And silent planets in the sky

Good fortune travels round and round
Just like this world where joy is found —

And in its circular racing track
It must someday perforce come back

And pass the spot on which you stand
And drop right in your friendly hand.

An Hour

Upon the shores of far Cathay
Down where the fiery dragons play
Where centuries pass as though a day
I rested on the sand —
Beneath the purple dome of night
Pierced by the star-world's glimmering light
Illuming Heaven's avenues bright
Along the Circling Band

A princess of this lotus land
Came — shared with me the cooling sand
And there I kissed her trembling hand
While meteors passed by —
She listened to my tales of old
Of valorous times when knights were bold —
The sweetest stories ever told
To fairest of the fair.

Then planets rolling into space
To watch the moon with smiling face
Glide past overshadowed in his race
Looked in upon us there —

While rumbling surf and sighing trees
Orchestral tones borne on the breeze
Re-echoed far above the seas
For one as sad as I —
Had I not come around the world

By ocean wave and typhoon hurled
With sails for Loveland rent and furled
But with a lover's message —
To pass in ships that sail by night
So many maidens in my plight
Of being ever doomed to flight
A lonesome bird of passage —

To find upon this distant shore
A maiden who hath ne'er before
Been loved by Love — and evermore
Earn not a lover's wages?
But lonesome souls if asked may say:
To love by night or love by day
When lovers know a lover's way
An hour may count for ages!

Desert Dreams

Here on the plains that nurtured barb'rous tribes.
Where Khans of Tartary were forced to fall,
When rule of Chow and all their worthy scribes
Gave way to Ch'in, the builder of the wall—

Bemusing what the Folks are thinking now
At Home, where routine fills the daily page—
Where generations through the years allow
Connected rounds of friends for every age—

Allured by Dame Adventure's gentle sway
The Gobi Desert only for my bed
I think like all who take the rover's way
And wonder if they mourn me with the dead—

I see the bees upon the blooming vine
Creep in and out the honeysuckle flower
And hum in tune with dreams that once
   were mine
To fill the days of youth—each golden hour—

I walk adown the lanes I learned to love
Where chestnut trees in Autumn shed their burrs
Beneath the leaves that rustled from above
To music of a voice that once was Hers—

I wonder if around me with Romance
The nieces and the nephews weave my name
As I of those whose absence did enhance
Their travels—O, I hope it is the same!

Whilst I'm enveloped by the screen of night
'Neath canopy of jewelled indigo
I hear the wild-geese honking in their flight
To warmer climes before the coming snow—

A dog now barks afrom another camp—
I feel the muffled breath of camels near—
The coolies play their cards beneath the lamp
And thus, I ask what comes within the year?

I wonder, do the lights of Milky Way
Reflect the souls of all the millions spent
In Asia, where the years are but a day
Of history, upon this continent!

I dreamt until once more I was a boy—
Familiar voices ringing in my ears—
A dozen school-mates entered to annoy
With capers, as they had in other years—

Then suddenly I learned that I was blind—
The darkness came upon me unawares—
My happiness was full—I did not mind—
I heard the tones I knew that once were Hers—

And with a loving kiss upon my hair
And fingers clasped with mine, like olden days
It mattered not were all the angels there —
Such ecstasy ne'er comes by other ways —

I struggled long and hard that I might see —
Add color to the voice that brought me joy —
Then shades of night rolled back their canopy
To show the worried visage of my "boy."

*   *   *

The Autumn rain has come on me at last
And beaten long upon my grizzled face —
My caravan is leaving — time has passed —
The dawn now marks the camel's measured pace —

The mud is deep and everything is wet —
The coolies dripping add but to the grime —
Such soggy chilled discomfort here, and yet
Romance it may be called — some future time.

Forbidden Fruit

Never judge
Of a book
By its cover:
This has been
Said before.

Nor a girl
By the halo
Above her,
If on a
Ball room floor.

*   *   *

A vision fair in old Peking
With eyes of desert blue
And when she danced a barb'ric fling
My senses upward flew.

To see a human form divine
Upon a rhythmic wave
Is more than words can well define
When nature won't behave.

My youth it craved just one caress
Of heaven's joy 'twould seem
To bask within the loveliness
Of such a sylphic dream.

Alas, thought I, 'tis Fancy's call—
Tomorrow I must go
Beyond the Manchu's famous wall
To Siber's dreary snow.

The caravan it leaves at dawn
With camels dignified;
Into the vastness I'll be drawn
With Thought alone my bride.

And lo, behold, the morning—basked
In smoke o'er all the town
Revealed a form befurred—who asked
To ride my camel brown—

Fair Katrinka of the floating dance—
The one of yester eve—
Who by some trick of Goddess Chance
Must take a hasty leave

From walled Peking through Nankau Pass
By caravan as old
As paths worn deep in rocks—alas,
With sorrows never told:

And so we rode—a pensive twain—
Beneath the Lama's Gate
Quite lazily our desert train
Played silently with Fate.

Upon the chords of my poor heart—
This maiden spoke the tongue
That eyes alone betray in part
When loving songs are sung—

Deep was her artist-soul, so full
Of love to satisfy
And make each hour more beautiful
To live and not to die.

Betimes she'd entertain me with
Old songs from Russian scribes—
Again she'd change with dash and wit
To tales of Tartar tribes.

And oft her smiles would drive me wild
To claim her for my bride
And then she'd feign a weeping child
To slip away and hide.

'Twas thus we played for days and days.
And nightly when she'd sleep
Her face would bless the desert haze
Through vigils I would keep.

One night more beautiful than all—
The shadow of the moon
Concealed a bandit's crew whose call
Raised pandemonium soon—

Within our camp, mid groans and shrieks
I dashed to save her life—
Was bound and gagged, then dawn's pale streaks
Revealed—the Chieftain's wife!

*   *   *

We see a plum,
A beauty—peach—
With eyes agleam
For it we reach—

It's fragrance calls
Us to our toes
And then it falls
To hit our nose-

And "Oh!" we sing—
Or else we cry:
"The rotten thing!"
And pass it by.

The Great Wall of China

With China's glory far behind,
Her splendor long bedimmed,
Here stands the work a master mind
Hath built, with human-limbed
Equipment in ye olden days
When brain and brawn were free
From steam and other modern ways—
This Great Wall to the sea.

Five hundred million yards of stone
With sand and lime and mortar fill,
Were borne by hands and feet alone
O'er valley, plain and hill—
Two thousand miles and many more
Of granite slabs and blocks
Were laid from China's eastern shore
To Tibet's lofty rocks.

A million of camels and of men,
With sheep and goats, and wives
Here toiled in hoards beyond our ken—
Old China's seething lives.
Here standing on this monument—
We ask the Gods of Time
To tell us how the Soul was spent
Of China in her prime.

The Story Teller

When Jack Frost was on the windows
And the winter nights were bleak
We would gather round and listen
When our Uncle Jeff would speak.

He would tell us tales of travel
Over mountains plains and sea.
And such tales as he'd unravel
Would enchant a child like me.

So please listen and I'll tell you
All about our Uncle J—
Who's the biggest and the kindest
Man in all the world today!

You may picture by your fire-side
His betanned and rugged face
As though chiseled from the mountains—
A true son of Nordic race—

With his high and noble forehead
And benevolent his chin—
And his merry little eyes that
Always twinkle from within—

With his ears set low and ample
He can hear the strangest sounds
Of the birds and beasts of jungles
When he makes his yearly rounds

Through the latitudes e'er changing
Upon either hemisphere
And o'er longitudes we sailed in
Merry tales with this old dear.

He would tell us of the monkey
That would tease the jaguar wild
Just to frighten him away from
Where the monkey kept his child—

How the jaguar fooled the monkey
By a cunning little ruse
And the monkey made a meal that
Ne'er a jaguar would refuse—

How in Tierra del Fuego
Or, in Chili and Peru
Or, way down in Patagonia
Were eagle hawks, he knew—

187

How the eagles watched the hunters
Of guanaco — and would greet
Every hunting party — trail them
For what hunters wouldn't eat —

How a very famous hunter
Stalked guanacos in a skin
Of another of their brothers
To conceal himself within —

Till a puma took the hunter
For guanaco one fine day —
As he slept within his make-up —
Now he stalks no more that way —

How a man in South Australia
Who though eighty years of age
Hunted dingo in the mountains
With a bounty for his wage —

How he got but one big dingo
In a month with battered gun
Took it thirty miles to get
Thirty shillings for his fun —

Till one cold and frosty morning
Came a woodman to the hills
Where he found the hunter smiling
Though quite dead from age and chills.

So will end the life of many
An old hunter in this world
Who will leave their sport a-smiling
When their toes are upward curled —

And I'm sure that Uncle Jeff will go
A-smiling with the brave
And ask for nothing better
Than a mountain for a grave.

SHAMUS A'RABBITT

Manchuria

(1924)

If from the East we come in through the door
Which opens to the arm of old Korea
And travel northward overland we'll find
The barren hills, from years of wasted lives,
Are being patched by thrifty Japanese
With pine and oak and other hardy trees—
Where waste and desolation of the past
Bestirred some two or more score years ago
By horny-handed rugged Western men
Who sunk their shafts and built the mountain flume
And opened to the torpid native mind
The light and life of Progress—with the rails
To reach the great Manchurian plains.

If through the Southern or the Western Gate
We reach the plains along the Yellow Sea
Or enter at the end of China's wall
Or, from the North through Siber's dreary snow
We find the pioneer hath left his bones
In silent spots amid the clustered stones—
The hardy ones whose lot it was to roam

Afar from kith and kin and friendly town
To come from many corners of our globe —
Afar from every homeside stream and field
Or country lane with memories filled
In unison with every season's mood.

Here staged upon the bleak Manchurian plain
Afar from all that Western men hold dear
We see the drama's drab and dreary course,
The slow and sluggish metal with its dross
E'er mixing and remixing to upbuild
An empire where but in the yesteryear
Through wind and sand the Mongol stunned by time
Was moving with a dull and bovine tread.

Here biting all the ugly dust and grime
We find the men of Nordic stock inured
To roughness of the blazers of the trail —
The man from north of Tweed, the hardy Scot
Who drifted over cold Siberian plains
Prospecting down the Ulya to Okotsk —
The man from Queensland who had trekked alone
Along the Andes searching gold
Or up the Rio de la Plat' to Corumba —
The one who built the plant that made the guns
Which drove the Russians backward from
     these plains —
Another browsed around the Philippines
To mix here with the fop just out from Home
Complaining o'er the absence of the Ritz,

Its perfume baths and dainty manicure —
The trader who will stay for weary years
To make a home on uncongenial soil,
A Western home in splendid isolation
Like the lotus gracing well the stagnant pool —
A flower in a sea of desolation.

What of the day prescribed by Time to come
When o'er these plains spring cities fair and great —
Will those who come to fill the banquet halls,
The fairy balls or drama on the stage —
To watch the manikins perform like all
Now here to toil and eat the dust and grime —
Will they who ride along the avenues green
Displaying charms — the fairest of the fair —
Will they — yes, all the dainty ones to come
Give but a single thought to these old dogs
Who struggle now to scratch the crusted earth
And turn the dross of rough hewn pavements gold?

The Passing of Old Landmarks

(IN MEMORIUM — 1923)

Appalling the sight to those
    who have seen it,
But saddest to those who far,
    far away
Are forced to submit to horrors
    of silence —
Intense is our mourning,
    though voiceless — we pray.

*   *   *

About the middle of a century
The gods hath blessed with their enlightenment,
Our hardy Western mariners were landed
Upon the fairest of Pacific isles —

So fair it seemed descended from the gods —
Its mountain slopes extending to the sea
With verdure ever green enkist by rain
From clouds that hugged the rugged
    mountain peaks —

193

Where mists through night e'er slept in valleys low
Supporting oft the crests of sacred hills,
Arresting eyes of e'en our hardy men—
With beauty that would soften hearts of oak—

Where art was part of every layman's life,
Where wants were few and comforts there
    were many—
A sylvan-like simplicity the rule
That each have time for meditative thought.

Where paper doors in straw-thatched cottages
With amber-glow like fire-flies in the night,
Sent forth their merry and yet plaintive sounds—
Vibrating koto, samisen and flute.

Where temple bells would moan the end of day
O'er sacred lichen-covered tombs where rest
The long departed great, the great as known
To stoical descendents of the East—

A static passive greatness much of thought
And needing union with the Western mind
For action, where but thought would pass away—
To raise the world a new and wonder child.

Our mariners here joined this old regime
And added they their Nordic sturdiness
To drop from time to time their hardy seeds
Of rugged and perennial Western trees:

The oak, the elm, the ash and maple too,
With tender saplings planted far from home
To fall on rocky soil and come to grief
In marshes of the Oriental lust.

But others they upon the soil took root
And over half a century have stood
As landmarks to the Westerners who climb
The latitudes of Asiatic shores —

Some noted for their stocky sturdiness,
Their solid trunks and character of Thor —
Trees of Albion benevolent of shade
Sweet gentleness e'er whispering through
    their leaves.

How oft old travellers basked in kindly light
And hospitality a-from the West
Transplanted to a foreign soil but true
To lands their ancestors helped to build.

And though they drank of scorching native suns
And breathed alien air of foster-land
They shed the glory and the blessings too
From stock of which their ancestry was proud.

Their friendships blest the isle of their adoption
And struggling through the springtime of their lives
Until acclimatized to Eastern world,
They reached their kindly autumn years of life.

From time to time they passed — these sentinels —
As silently as morn enfolds the mist
And one by one no longer graced the shores —
Horizon of this once enchanted isle.

With passing of these soldiers brave, of time,
Our gratefulness enhanced those left behind —
Woe, therefore, unto us Old Eastern Hands
When wrath of Gods of Quake and Fire and Wave

Hath lashed in such a fury as to take
These staunch old Beacon Lights and rugged trees —
Our friends, the landmarks of the Isle of Fans —
What purpose hath the Gods — leave us behind?

> Our prayers to God of Good
> we pour —
> Our hope for those who've
> gone before
> Our comrades of the days
> no more —
> We'll meet upon a
> friendly shore.

Wine of Human Kindness

I often wonder when I drink
About the mists on what I think—
If all the haloes that I see
Are phantoms or reality—
With one or two good drinks within
The world about me has no sin—
A maiden's smile is like a flower—
All trouble passes like a shower
To leave me calm as is the day
When summer rains have passed away—
Of course I know long faces who
Will say that wine no good can do
But I remember as a boy
When Scriptures brought to me their joy
Of happiness for all mankind
One thing imprest upon my mind
Was how the Good Lord with his band
Would call for wine to bless the land
And drink with all Disciples true
Before He told them what He knew.

Please Come Again

The weather is "unusual"
When e'er a stranger reaches town—
In London, Paris, or New York—
Or other places of renown—
"You should have come a month ago—
You should be here when we have snow—
You would enjoy our season's rain
If you could but a month remain—"
Oh, I am wondering if ever I
Can reach Japan when it is dry—
In California never yet
Have I arrived when it was wet—
I wonder if when I reach Hell
Old Nick will say I've not done well
To come when all the fires are out
And tell me I should turn about.
And come again for earthly reasons
When Hell is in the best of seasons.

Ode to Lady Bountiful

Not from a poet
Not from a lark
Not from an owl
Who sees in the dark —
Not from an eagle
That soars up on high
Not from a wild goose
That honks through the sky —

Not from a maiden
Whose heart has been stilled
With love she was cravin'
Before it was filled —
Not from a bachelor
Sitting at ease
With no one to bother him —
No one to please —

Not from a millionaire
Cold and forlorn
Who sees gold in the sunrise
Instead of the morn —
Not from anything
That you could conceive
This grateful ode's written
For Heaven's reprieve —

Not written from sadness
My lot to bemoan
But written in gladness
From my heart alone
To tell of the rescue
Of a sorrowful bird
From a life of such darkness
You never have heard—

Not darkness of evening
Not darkness of night
But darkness of everything
Happy and bright.

*   *   *

Yes—I was a prisoner
With only the stars
Of an alien country
To shine through the bars—
Attended by savages
Who spoke not my tongue—
The language of sailors
That caressed me when young—

Until by God's graces
In late thirty-eight
'Mid millions of faces
That passed by my gate
There came a kind lady
With a heart full of love

For birds in their cages —
A voice from above —

A voice full of music
From a life full of fun —
A voice full of gladness
As warm as the sun —
Whose "good-morning" was
    wine —
Whose "good-day" was song —
Whose kindness was pulling
This old world along —

As I've told you already
She stopped at my gate.
And changed the whole world
Of my horrible state —
From madness to gladness —
From wildness to love
She changed me with mildness
From parrot to dove —

Yes — truth it will finally
Find its way out —
By now you will know
What this is about —
'Tis just an old parrot
Who's trying to tell
How a bountiful lady
Has pulled him from Hell —

*   *   *

She found me a home
And found me a master—
A mistress as well
To make my days faster—

Named for my lady
I'll make her amends
To merit my name
Of Mr. Florenze—
     "Polly love Master—
     Polly love Missie"
Is what I will say
But I am no sissy—

I'm now in a port
Where ships come and go—
Where sailors are singing
The songs that I know—
The songs that are music
To one who has heard
The language that's suited
To a blasphemous bird.

Rainbow Chasers

We travel abroad to find
Adventure to fill the mind
Through hours and days
With wonderment —
Exotic ways.

When a thousand leagues
From home —
Increased a thousand more
By time — we roam
O'er lands that smell
Unlike our own —
With sounds well
Nigh unknown
To us —
Our ancestors —
Our race —
We then see palaces
In our old home place.

We treasure what
We've left behind
And wonder how
We were so blind
As to leave the
Old town's country lane—
The hicks that used
To cause us pain—
The poor relations
Needing dough
And everyone we used to know.

Resolved are we
When home—
We'll go
To every concert
Every show—
At the opera
We'll have a box
At every race
A seat—
To every night club
Take our girl—
By jove—but we'll
Be in the whirl.

Old friends
New loves will be—
All our relatives
We'll see.

Oh, what a thousand leagues
From home will do —
We treasure
What our native shore
Possesses that we
Never knew before!

* * *

So home we go to old time friends
Who've changed a thousand ways
From those we knew and honored in
Our young and carefree days —

We wonder why we left the sights
And scenes of foreign lands —
Mysterious Oriental nights
On fascinating strands —

We wonder why the other side
Seems smooth on every road
And why our burden's heavier than
The other fellow's load —

* * *

Dilemma always has two horns —
We choose the smoothest fit —
But horns we pass n'er look as, sharp
As those on which we sit.

SHAMUS A'RABBITT

In Defense of Nonsense

I admire
The monk within
The cloistered cell
Who lives
For his salvation—
But to me his life
Would be a hell
I'd much prefer
Starvation.

The banker in
His gilded cage
Must live
By counting what
Intrigues me not—
I prefer to rage
With friends
O'er what I haven't got.

The men of science
I admire—
To me
They are the saints
Who've rescued men
From fear of fire—
Rid life
Of dire complaints.

But when
The beaker's empty and

When the flask
Is cold
And cobwebs
Close laboratories —
Men
Will still grow old —

Grow old
And lose their vigour
For enjoyment
And for fun —
Collapse
From winter's rigour —
Collapse
From burning sun —

O, God give me
The midway course
Between
Religion, science, art —
And mix my life
With work and love —
My mind
Guide by my heart.

And when I go
I hope there'll be
A few who'll laugh
And smile for me
And think me not
Devoid of sense
Because I've written
This defense.

SHAMUS A'RABBITT

The Forgotten Man

Public Sap Number One
Believed in everybody —

To him no one
Could do a wrong —

He sung the praises
Of mankind, places, friends —

His enemies he knew not —
Contented ever with his lot —

With head immersed he walked
Within the clouds and talked

With man, woman, maid and child
Savants, statesmen, bums and kings —

Alas we ring for him the bell
That tolls for those who picture hell

A place where briquetted roses grow
And fragrant souls forever glow

With pride and joy and sing within
Without the consciousness of sin —

The tolling bells will die away
As we return and end the day

We buried him who'd cared not a rap
That he was Number One — the Public Sap.

The Forgotten Woman

Cold and austere
(Outwardly at least)
She walked —
With her head to the heavens.

Straight on her path
(As far as we knew)
Of duty —
Her watchword was promptness.

She weighed all matters
(With the caution
Of a judge —)
In her shrewdness —

A place for all things
(Except kissing)
And all things in their place —
Was her motto —

Slow to forget
(In strength of opinion)
Unyielding to wrong
Was her virtue.

A princess
(Or, goddess —)
A queen do you ask —
Or, perchance a martyr?

Nay, e'en more
(Than all of these)
Was she —
In her stronghold.

She was just Sister May
(Misnamed from the seasons)
Twixt winter and summer —
For ne'er does she bud in the springtime.

Gibraltar — a monument
To that which is stable and staid —
In grandeur, perfection —
A healthy old-maid.

A Beachcomber's Lament

A million dollars have I not—
On easy street I have no lot
And though I never whine or sob
I haven't even got a job.

I trudge along on weary feet—
And pass the shops on every street
Their windows filled with Christmas joys
To bring good cheer to girls and boys.

Ten thousand gems and I have none—
A million homes—for me not one—
The dough I had is now all gone—
Not left one sou for wine or song.

There's just one thing I wish I had
To swell my heart and make me glad—
Just one wee post card I could send
To my old pal—my dear old friend.

SHAMUS A'RABBITT

Magnificence of Failure

Dreams, just dreams
Adventurous dreams —
I've worked and I've played
Caroused in the dance —
For fame I haven't
A ghost of a chance.

I've traveled and found
In volumes of old
In dusty gray libraries
Nuggets of gold —

Rare gems of wisdom
That history has wrought
From ancients who lived
By deeds and by thought.

The fortunes I've made —
The fortunes I've lost —
Were worth all the effort —
Were worth all the cost!

O, God, how I've lived —
How I've gambled with life —
E'er winning the bet —
Magnificent my failures —
And still not dead yet!

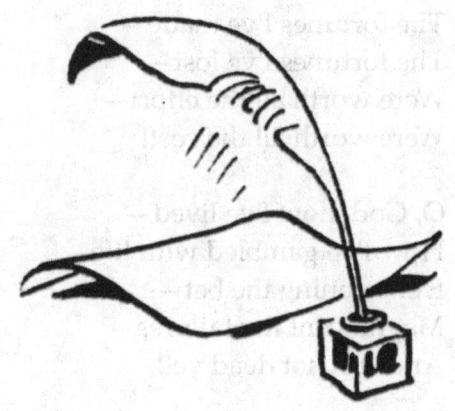

Resolutions

Once more we've raced
Around the track
Of years that pass
And ne'er come back.

Once more resolved
To do our bit
The better if
We die for it.

Once more resolved
To write a book
That all the world
May read and look

To brighter things
Within our soul
Than heretofore
Hath been its goal.

Once more we swear
That on our way
We'll never fail
Our "line-a-day"

And so we start
In to indite
That line a day
Which we must write

The same as we
Have done before
And burned our diaries
By the score.

SHAMUS A'RABBITT

The Swan-song of a Refugee (1924)

I came upon an autumn breeze
To sing for all the refugees —
A bird equipped with broken wing
A broken purse and everything.

Then lo, behold! By my ovation
The Times increased its circulation —
While other local papers lost
All their subscribers at their cost.

I lost the prize of Mr. Bok
And so in peace I take no stock
While still I have a world to shake
With pen and ink like fire and quake.

Although my nerves are shaky yet
My monthly bills they must be met
And now there isn't one Red — (Cross)
To compensate me for my loss.

The wolf now scratches at my door
As he hath scratched poets before —
O, fool — I did not use the kind
Of varnish that no wolf could find!

And Oh, alas! though dreaming's nice
I now must earn my fish and rice —
I'll go to work — 'tis sad but true
That I may eat as coolies do.

A poet's pay is not enough —
I'm tired of all this "glory" stuff —
To answer all the men of state
My cable bills are very great:

They're all congratulating me
For my inspiring poetry —
E'en Kipling, Shaw and many more
Have sent me letters by the score.

Of course they're jealous of my work —
I find within their praises lurk
Their envy of my genius rare —
Which I'll admit's beyond compare.

So, good-bye readers one and all
I hear the snapping wolflets call
To take from death its awful sting
By starving one who'll write and sing!

And so henceforth you will be free
From driveling lines like these from me —
Lines of a singing refugee
In syncopated poetry.

When We Go Sailing Home

PRELUDE

Last night while in my narrow bed
I scratched the hair all off my head
Until my brains were wholly porous
For rhymes to suit my farewell chorus.

At last I hit upon a plan
To write for children maid and man
Especially those who like to roam —
About — WHEN WE GO SAILING HOME.

*   *   *

OVERTURE

How dull it must be
For the old bargee
Who will at home remain —
But lucky are we
Who've sailed the sea
And soon will sail again!

*   *   *

Ting-a-ling-ling! Up goes the curtain!

218

LEAVE TAKING

At last the time has come for HOME—
In dreams of sultry nights
We've longed for homeside hills to roam
Through fancy's wildest flights!

Now, dinners, cards and chits, no more—
We sell whate'er we own—
For stern views of old Asia's shore,
To some a joy unknown.

We send our P. P. C.'s around—
The tidings to apprise—
And then forgotten chits are found
To furnish a Surprise—

AND HOW!

BON VOYAGE

Great days will always come at last—
With friends we now repair—
To sail away with steamer's blast
And "good byes" in the air.

HONGKONG SING SONG

I don't know
The song the sailor sings
When the sailor's a dark Chinese —
It sounds like a song
A sailor sings —
A ribald song of the seas.

Perhaps if put
In English words
'Twould lose its salty smell
'Twould lose its swing
And lusty ring
Of devils down in hell.

Perhaps it's but
A "woman" song
That's sung by men of the sea
That's sung whenever
They leave a port
Or wherever they may be —

For even a Chinaman's
Fantan lust
And long days in the hold
Cannot put down
The call of the dust
That calls today
As of old.

Perhaps it is only
A sing song chant
That longs for a moment of bliss—
Whatever it is I do not know
But it sounds a lot like this:

Hongkong is an island in
The Southern China Sea
Where dusky maidens smile and
The sing song girls are free.

The sing song girls in China are
A-beckoning to me
From Hongkong and Eastern Asia
From tropic isles and sea.

Hongkong girls are Hongkong pearls
As dusky as can be
For Hongkong is an island in
The Southern China Sea.

Where green hills rise from ocean and
The blue skies meet them there—
Where nights are filled with music and
There's mystery in the air.

Where stars hang from the heavens and
Where song is in the air
Five seas are turned to seven and
Old Hongkong calls me there.

THE BRINY DEEP

Once more we're out upon the sea
The world revolves for us
And think we now how great to be
A conquering hero thus.

We change and dress that we may dine
And have a drink or two
And tell the steward about our wine
But this twixt me and you!

The Jolly Steward

Oh, jolly is the steward and
Our lives are now care-free
He's opened up his medicine
That's good for one at sea —

We'll tell you his prescription and
Pray ever shall it be —
Cocktails at noon not more than six —
At night not less than three —

And through the day no limit to
The soda we may take —
Of course there's something in it if
'Tis just for old time's sake —

And so the world looks brighter and
We now can write once more —
In jocund vein and lighter than
We ever could before

Stop! Look!! Loosen!!!

HARK! HARK! The Deck Poet stutters
With fountain pen he spumes and sputters
With facile nib and nimble wit
He's happy if he makes a hit —
                    (with the ladies).

Come loosen belts and let your ribs expand
For mirth-provoking Shamus Rabbitt's hand
Is busy making rhyming quips anew
To please himself if never pleasing you.

Lazy Days

O, lazy days they'll always be
The first few days we spend at sea —
To doze and read and sleep and gaze
At those who smile at us these days.

'Neath cloudless skies — or overcast
With heavy streaks that scurry past —
We sail and watch the sky and sea
Where the horizon line should be.

With breezes soft and perfume laden
As soothing as the breath of maiden —
We see the sun perform his best
Of miracles and go to rest.

The moon with beams to gleam at night
Always so intimate a sight —
He sends them down a golden street
Forever dancing to our feet.

We cease to dream and settle down
When all hands lose their deadly frown —
A smile or two and lo, behold!
Come friendly greedngs — young and old!

SHAMUS A'RABBITT

Man Overboard

Man overboard! Throw him a smile!
How happy we'd be
When sailing the sea,
If lives could be saved by throwing a smile.

Man overboard! Throw him a smile!
'Tis something to know
Wherever we go
That lives may be saved by spending a smile.

Chimes O'the Sea

I love
The chimes of Normandy —
The tolling chimes
Of Trinity —
St. Paul's sweet chimes
Appeal to me —
But of
All chimes
Please God give me
Chow chimes
Three times
Each day
At sea.

Tales O'the Sea

'Tis strange that all our tales of sea
Are of ye olden days —
"Before the mast" no more can be
But what about our ways?

We read that in the days of yore
Ye olden Jolly Rogers
Amused themselves with blood and gore
Of laws were artful dodgers —

And too along the China coast
Those days the wooden ships
Were manned by men of iron who'd boast
Of many fearsome trips.

A Whale of a Jonah

We never thought that we would be
A jonah on a smiling sea —
We never thought our lines would shake
The sides of all until they'd break —
Yes, even boilers in the ship
They shook until their tubes did slip
The siren laughed until 'twas hoarse
And then the captain lost his course —
To Yokohama turned our prow
And that is where we're going now
Unless again from lines like these
That we are writing on the seas
Old jonah wakens from his sleep
With Neptune in the briny deep
And springs on us a happy leak
That may delay us for a week —

Ohio De Gozaimasu! Irashai!

A voyage on the deep blue ocean
Leaves few if any on the trip
Who haven't got at least a notion
Of WHO is WHO upon the ship.

Most folk would we
Not like to be
But then we nearly
Always see
That those who are
So virtuous
Are surely modelled
After us.

230

As We See Others

To while away the time now We
Will rhyme the passengers we see —
Our list you'll find about the same
On every ship with any name.

Begins with one whose art at cards
Is heard by seamen on the yards —
A language shark from Tokyo
Will practice "So ka? I don't know!"

And then "the sweet and pretty thing"
Of her in rapture we might sing —
Her eyes her lips her sculptured hair
And gowns that maketh females stare.

And then the happy bride and groom
Who spoon upon their honeymoon
Until we come to leave the ship —
From passports many truths will slip.

You know the bird who sings success
But when we land is in distress
And touches you for just a few —
The same old game — what can you do?

And then the dear old man in grey
Who's in the corner every day
And reads his book so meek and mild —
He is the great Sir Joseph Wild.

Somewhat unlike the great big king
Who leads the sports and everything —
Who puts on side and tries to sing —
He travels for the whiskey ring.

Our paupers dress e'en to their ears
With diamonds look like millionaires
And millionaires they go threadbare
To get their portion everywhere.

You've met old grouch the son of gloom
Who'll tell you how there is no room
For any ships of any types
To fly aloft the Stars and Stripes?

Now if it happens that you are
Just born beneath a happy star
Beware and give Old Grouch some room
Or he'll consign you to your doom.

And now we'll dose this rotten verse
Before they put us in a hearse —
All hail — the worthies — let us cheer
Our passengers are not all here!

Old Cap Says!

On windy days
When lightly laden
With silk and trifles
Loved by ladies
Our ship takes kindly
To the seas —
Sails sprightly
Blithesome
As a maiden —
But
When she's loaded
To the gun'als
With iron and steel
That men love well
She groans and creaks
And ploughs the seas
A quiver
A shiver
To rattle like hell.

The Fair Pacific

Balboa climbed upon a hill
One calm and peaceful day —
'Tis said he got a glorious thrill
Alone so far away. —

Old Bal he had a lot of sight
But not enough by day
To reach across — so he looked at night
And saw a peaceful bay.

He called the bay an ocean and
With smiles quite beatific —
The waters were so blue and calm —
He named them fair Pacific.

And in the bottle from his hip
A sample soon he took
And sent it back for Spain to sip
And record in a book —

Father Neptune

All those who climb the latitudes
To cross Equator's line
Or East and West on longitudes
Must pay Old Neptune's fine.

This great good king rules under sea —
Takes toll on lines Meridian
Though calm or rough the seas may be
We meet this great comedian!

With mermaiden daughter fair —
The queen of all the seas —
He sits in state with hempen hair
That curls about his knees —

And e'en his crown be made of tin
His robe of table cloth
You'll feel his briny imprint in
Your goose-flesh when you're caught.

His retinue made up of men
The oldest of our crew
Strike terror to all mortals when
They look them through and through —

Saucepans for helmets on their heads
For shields the lids of pots
And flowing mantles — spreads from beds —
Sustained by sailor's knots —

For sword each carries a Gillette
To pierce the hearts of those
Who will of deep sea justice get
When Neptune blows his nose.

But Neptune cannot work when dry
As he lives in the sea —
For more and more good wine he'll cry
And he must have it free.

So on the day we cross the line
We make the victims weep
As each one pays old Neptune's fine
In the Order of the Deep.

The Wayside Isles

On every voyage
One may take
'Tis well that there
Should be a break.

So on this broad
Pacific basin
'Tis well to stop
At some way station.

To fill your gas tanks
And what is more
To see what pranks
Are played on shore.

So listen friends—
What e'er you do
We recommend
Hon-o-lu-lu.

Isles of Liquid Sunshine

I roam beneath the palm trees
Down by the rolling sea
Where sweet caressing balm-breeze
Comes wafting o'er the lea
To trace upon the sand piles
With scintillating spray
Rare liquid-sunshine-land-smiles
In dreamland of the lei.

Along the sun-baked reaches
Day-dreaming here I roam —
Like birds on wave-raped beaches
Come surf-boats on the foam
Where swimming, native figures, browned
Are singing in the sun
Soft melodies of plaintive sound
With waves in unison.

Upon a dusky bronzed maiden
I see a string of shells
With tropic blossoms perfume laden
Tossed on the ocean swells —
I barter with the maiden fair
Whose smiles of lips and eyes
Reflect the sunlight on her hair
Outdazzling opal skies —

What recompense, my pretty miss,
To give this string to me?
She answers softly — "But a kiss!" —
And plunges in the sea.

*　　*　　*　　*　　*

Did I obtain
The maiden's treasure-
Each iridescent shell — ?
Indeed, I did!
It now gives pleasure —
To whom?
I'll never tell!

Farewell to our Steamer

It's farewell to our steamer
(Her captain — staff — and seamen)
A sturdy ship, and proud are we
To have such vessels on the sea —

As all great voyages must end
We're soon to land and homeward wend
Our ways to towns both far and near,
But first we'll give a rousing cheer.

To master mariner and crew
Of the best ship we ever knew —
Come let us cheer them one and all
And thank them for the Captain's ball.

The Captain's Ball

With music and with sayings bright
We dined and danced till past midnight,
And after that the midnight air
Was rent with noise beyond compare,
To wildest freaks all were inclined
Enough to paralyse the mind!

And later too some stayed we think
To greet the morning with a drink,
But say all those who ought to know
They stopped to sing a song or so —
All night we heard them strain their necks
To serenade us from the decks.

Land Ahoy!

A song of scent
As pungent as
The salt spray
From the sea
Came from the throats
Of the sailors as
We pulled
Around the lea—
Then downward went
The anchor and
The chain—
It clanked and fell
Into the briny depths
As bottomless as hell.

Home Again

Home from Far Eastern shores
To bustle smoke and grind—
Aromas that here greet us
All savor of our kind—

The very earth gives welcome—
We're soon enveloped in
The speeding and the going
As well as in the din.

We call on Tried and Trusty
Our friends of bygone days—
They're gone or worse—are married—
Have had to mend their ways.

And then we sit and listen
The CALL it comes again
And tells us what we're missing
If we at home remain:
               LISTEN!

The Lure of the East

O, what is the call
That comes to us all
When once we have been in the EAST —
To lure us away
For life and a day
In tropics to rot in the EAST.

Away from our fields
Where no harvest yields
A fragrance on which we may FEAST —
No walks in the woods
With trees and their moods
No orchards to bloom in the EAST —

No strolls by the streams
Where tropic sun gleams
No skylarks to sing in the EAST —
No welcome within
A countryside inn
Not out in old Asia at LEAST!

We roam o'er the lands
With sweat on our hands
Discomfort for man and for BEAST —
The mildew's a fright
On boots overnight
'Tis muggy and damp in the EAST —

Where roaches eat books
And lizards from nooks
Will sport on our walls in the EAST —
Where snakes and the ants
Will sleep in our pants
And flies on our food make a FEAST —

It rains and it rains
Till blocking our drains
For sewers we've none in the EAST —
A "symphony" of smell
No language can tell
But yet we return to the EAST —

To filth we are blind
Benumbed is the mind
But still we go back to the EAST —
We call in at Cook's
And are happy he books
To where LOVE — is the love of the
    EAST!